FAST
Grade 8 Math Practice

GET DIGITAL ACCESS TO

 2 FAST Practice Tests

 Personalized Study Plans

REGISTER NOW

Important Instruction

Register online using the link and the access code provided by your teacher.

Enter the access code (for your reference) in the box given below.

Access Code:

FAST Online Assessments and 8th Grade Math Practice Workbook, Student Copy

Contributing Editor - Nicole Fernandez
Contributing Editor - Nancy Chang
Contributing Editor - Greg Applegate
Executive Producer - Mukunda Krishnaswamy
Program Director - Anirudh Agarwal
Designer and Illustrator - Sowmya R.

ISBN 13: 979-8357721778

Printed in the United States of America

CONTACT INFORMATION

LUMOS INFORMATION SERVICES, LLC

 PO Box 1575, Piscataway, NJ 08855-1575
 www.LumosLearning.com

 Email: support@lumoslearning.com
 Tel: (732) 384-0146
Fax: (866) 283-6471

Lumos Learning
Step Up Your Skills

INTRODUCTION

This book is specifically designed to improve student achievement on the Florida Assessment of Student Thinking (FAST). Students perform at their best on standardized tests when they feel comfortable with the test content as well as the test format. Lumos online practice tests are meticulously designed to mirror the state assessment. They adhere to the guidelines provided by the state for the number of sessions and questions, standards, difficulty level, question types, test duration and more.

Based on our decade of experience developing practice resources for standardized tests, we've created a dynamic system, the Lumos Smart Test Prep Methodology. It provides students with realistic assessment rehearsal and an efficient pathway to overcoming each proficiency gap.

Use the Lumos Smart Test Prep Methodology to achieve a high score on the FAST.

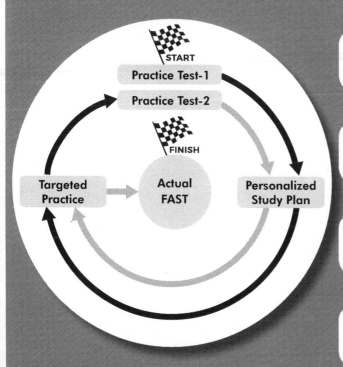

Lumos Smart Test Prep Methodology

START
Practice Test-1
Practice Test-2
FINISH
Targeted Practice   Actual FAST   Personalized Study Plan

1 The student takes the first online diagnostic test, which assesses proficiency levels in various standards.

2 StepUp generates a personalized online study plan based on the student's performance.

3 The student completes targeted practice in the printed workbook and marks it as complete in the online study plan.

4 The student then attempts the second online practice test.

5 StepUp generates a second individualized online study plan.

6 Additional activities are planned to help the student gain comprehensive mastery for success on the FAST.

Table of Contents

Chapter 1
Number Sense and Operations

Lesson 1: Rational vs Irrational Numbers

1. Which of the following is an integer?

Ⓐ -3
Ⓑ $\frac{1}{4}$
Ⓒ -12.5
Ⓓ 0.454545...

2. Which of the following statements is true?

Ⓐ Every rational number is an integer.
Ⓑ Every whole number is a rational number.
Ⓒ Every irrational number is a natural number.
Ⓓ Every rational number is a whole number.

3. Which of the following accurately describes the square root of 10?

Ⓐ It is rational.
Ⓑ It is irrational.
Ⓒ It is an integer.
Ⓓ It is a whole number.

4. Complete the following statement: Pi is _____ .

Ⓐ both real and rational
Ⓑ real but not rational
Ⓒ rational but not real
Ⓓ neither real nor rational

5. Complete the following statement: $\sqrt{7}$ is _____ .

Ⓐ both a real and a rational number
Ⓑ a real number, but not rational
Ⓒ a rational number, but not a real number
Ⓓ neither a real nor a rational number

6. The number 57 belongs to which of the following set(s) of numbers?

   Ⓐ **N only**
   Ⓑ **N, W, and Z only**
   Ⓒ **N, W, Z, and Q only**
   Ⓓ **All of the following: N, W, Z, Q, and R**

7. From the following set: {-√5.7, -9, 0, 5.25, 3i, √16}
   Select the answer choice that shows the elements which are Natural numbers.

   Ⓐ -√5.7, -9, 0, 5.25, 3i, √16
   Ⓑ -√5.7, -9, 0, 5.25, 3i
   Ⓒ 3i
   Ⓓ Positive square root of 16

8. From the following set: {-√5.7, -9, 0, 5.25, 3i, √16}
   Select the answer choice that shows the elements that are Rational numbers.

   Ⓐ -√5.7, -9, 0, 5.25, 3i, √16
   Ⓑ -9, 0, 5.25, √16
   Ⓒ 3i
   Ⓓ -√5.7

9. Which of the numbers below is irrational?

   Ⓐ √169
   Ⓑ √4
   Ⓒ √16
   Ⓓ √3

10. Write the repeating rational number 0.1515... as a fraction.

   Ⓐ $\dfrac{85}{100}$

   Ⓑ $\dfrac{15}{75}$

   Ⓒ $\dfrac{15}{99}$

   Ⓓ $\dfrac{25}{50}$

11. Write the repeating rational number .112112... as a fraction.

Ⓐ $\dfrac{112}{100}$

Ⓑ $\dfrac{112}{99}$

Ⓒ $\dfrac{112}{999}$

Ⓓ $\dfrac{111}{999}$

12. Which of the following is true of the square root of 2?

Ⓐ It is both real and rational.
Ⓑ It is real but not rational.
Ⓒ It is rational but not real.
Ⓓ It is neither real nor rational.

13. Which of the following sets includes the square root of -25?

Ⓐ R, Z, W, N, and Q
Ⓑ R, W, Q
Ⓒ Z, N
Ⓓ None of the above.

14. Complete the following statement:
The number 6.25 belongs to _____.

Ⓐ R, Q, Z, W, and N
Ⓑ R and Q
Ⓒ R and N
Ⓓ Q and Z

15. Complete the sentence:
Irrational numbers may always be written as _____.

Ⓐ fractions
Ⓑ fractions and as decimals
Ⓒ decimals but not as fractions
Ⓓ neither decimals or fractions

16. Which of the following are rational numbers?

Instruction : Mark all the correct options. More than one option may be correct.

Ⓐ $\dfrac{5}{7}$

Ⓑ $\sqrt{10}$

Ⓒ $\sqrt{25}$

Ⓓ π

17. Mark whether each number is rational or irrational.

	Rational	Irrational
$\sqrt{2}$		
$\dfrac{1}{3}$		
0.575		
$\dfrac{\sqrt{12}}{4}$		

18. Identify the irrational number and circle it.

Ⓐ $\dfrac{5}{7}$

Ⓑ 0.1

Ⓒ $\sqrt{10}$

CHAPTER 1 → Lesson 2: Approximating Irrational Numbers

1. Between which two whole numbers does $\sqrt{5}$ lie on the number line?

   Ⓐ 1 and 2
   Ⓑ 2 and 3
   Ⓒ 3 and 4
   Ⓓ 4 and 5

2. Between which pairs of rational numbers does $\sqrt{5}$ lie on the number line?

   Ⓐ 2.0 and 2.1
   Ⓑ 2.1 and 2.2
   Ⓒ 2.2 and 2.3
   Ⓓ 2.3 and 2.4

3. Order the following numbers on a number line (least to greatest).

   Ⓐ 1.8, 1.35, 2.5, $\sqrt{5}$
   Ⓑ 1.35, $\sqrt{5}$, 1.8, 2.5
   Ⓒ 1.35, 1.8, $\sqrt{5}$, 2.5
   Ⓓ 1.35, 1.8, 2.5, $\sqrt{5}$

4. If you fill in the _____ in each of the following choices with $\sqrt{7}$, which displays the correct ordering from least to greatest?

   Ⓐ ___, 2.5, 2.63, 2.65
   Ⓑ 2.5, ___, 2.63, 2.65
   Ⓒ 2.5, 2.63, ___, 2.65
   Ⓓ 2.5, 2.63, 2.65, ___

5. Which of the following numbers has the least value?

   Ⓐ $\sqrt{(0.6561)}$
   Ⓑ 0.8
   Ⓒ 0.8...
   Ⓓ 0.8884

6. Choose the correct order (least to greatest) for the following real numbers.

   Ⓐ $\sqrt{5}$, $4\frac{1}{2}$, 4.75, $2\sqrt{10}$

   Ⓑ $4\frac{1}{2}$, $\sqrt{5}$, $2\sqrt{10}$, 4.75

   Ⓒ $4\frac{1}{2}$, 4.75, $\sqrt{5}$, $2\sqrt{10}$

   Ⓓ $\sqrt{5}$, $2\sqrt{10}$, $4\frac{1}{2}$, 4.75

7. Which of the following numbers has the greatest value?

   Ⓐ 0.4...
   Ⓑ 0.444
   Ⓒ $\sqrt{0.4}$
   Ⓓ 0.45

8. Which of the following is ordered correctly from least to greatest?

   Ⓐ $\sqrt{0.9}$, 0.9, 0.999, 0.9...
   Ⓑ 0.9, $\sqrt{0.9}$, 0.999, 0.9...
   Ⓒ 0.9, 0.9..., $\sqrt{0.9}$, 0.999
   Ⓓ 0.9, 0.9..., 0.999, $\sqrt{0.9}$

9. Write the following numbers from least to greatest.

   Ⓐ $\sqrt{2}$, π, $3\frac{7}{8}$, $\frac{32}{8}$

   Ⓑ π, $\sqrt{2}$, $3\frac{7}{8}$, $\frac{32}{8}$

   Ⓒ $3\frac{7}{8}$, π, $\sqrt{2}$, $\frac{32}{8}$

   Ⓓ $\frac{32}{8}$, $3\frac{7}{8}$, π, $\sqrt{2}$

10. If you were to arrange the following numbers on the number line from least to greatest, which one would be last?

Ⓐ 3.6

Ⓑ $3\dfrac{7}{12}$

Ⓒ $\sqrt{12}$

Ⓓ $3\dfrac{9}{10}$

11. Between which of these pairs of rational numbers does $\sqrt{24}$ lie on the number line?

Ⓐ 4.79 and $4\dfrac{7}{8}$

Ⓑ $4\dfrac{7}{8}$ and 5.0

Ⓒ 4.95 and 5.0

Ⓓ 4.75 and 4.79

12. Between which two integers does $\sqrt{2}$ lie on the number line?

Ⓐ 0 and 1
Ⓑ 1 and 2
Ⓒ 2 and 3
Ⓓ 3 and 4

13. Between which pair of rational numbers does $\sqrt{2}$ lie on the number line?

Ⓐ 1.40 and 1.41
Ⓑ 1.41 and 1.42
Ⓒ 1.42 and 1.43
Ⓓ 1.43 and 1.44

14. Between which pair of consecutive integers on the number line does $\sqrt{3}$ lie?

Ⓐ 1 and 2
Ⓑ 2 and 3
Ⓒ 3 and 4
Ⓓ 4 and 5

15. Between which of the following pairs of rational numbers on the number line does √3 lie?

   Ⓐ 1.70 and 1.71
   Ⓑ 1.71 and 1.72
   Ⓒ 1.72 and 1.73
   Ⓓ 1.73 and 1.74

CHAPTER 1 → Lesson 3: Properties of Exponents

1. Is -5^2 equal to $(-5)^2$?

    (A) Yes, because they both equal -25.
    (B) Yes, because they both equal -10.
    (C) Yes, because they both equal 25.
    (D) No, because -5^2 equals -25 and $(-5)^2$ equals 25.

2. $\dfrac{X^6}{X^{-2}} =$

    (A) $\dfrac{1}{X^3}$

    (B) $\dfrac{1}{X^{12}}$

    (C) X^4

    (D) X^8

3. Which of the following is equal to 3^{-2} ?

    (A) $\dfrac{1}{9}$

    (B) -9

    (C) 9

    (D) $\dfrac{1}{6}$

4. Which of the following is equivalent to $X^{(2-5)}$?

    (A) X^3

    (B) $X^{\frac{1}{3}}$

    (C) $\dfrac{1}{X^3}$

    (D) 3^X

5. $1^9 =$

    Ⓐ 1
    Ⓑ 3
    Ⓒ 9
    Ⓓ $\dfrac{1}{9}$

6. $(X^{-3})(X^{-3}) =$

    Ⓐ X^6
    Ⓑ X^9
    Ⓒ $\dfrac{1}{X^6}$
    Ⓓ $\dfrac{1}{X^9}$

7. $(X^{-2})^{-7} =$

    Ⓐ X^5

    Ⓑ X^{14}

    Ⓒ $\dfrac{1}{X^5}$

    Ⓓ $\dfrac{1}{X^{14}}$

8. $(X^4)^0 =$

    Ⓐ X
    Ⓑ X^4
    Ⓒ 1
    Ⓓ 0

9. $(3^2)^3 =$

Ⓐ 3^5
Ⓑ 3^6
Ⓒ 3
Ⓓ 1

10. $5^2 + 5^3 =$ _____

11. Which of the following show the proper laws of exponents?

   Note : More than one option may be correct. Select all the correct answers.

   Ⓐ $3^2 \times 3^5 = 3^{10}$
   Ⓑ $(4^2)^3 = 4^6$
   Ⓒ $\dfrac{8^5}{8^1} = 8^4$
   Ⓓ $7^4 \times 7^4 = 7^8$

12. Simplify this expression.
   $a^7(a^8)(a)$

   Write your answer in the box below.

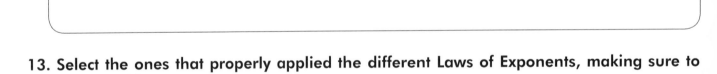

13. Select the ones that properly applied the different Laws of Exponents, making sure to keep positive exponents.

   Note : More than one option may be correct. Select all the correct answers.

   Ⓐ $(4a^3)^2 = 16a^6$
   Ⓑ $(2x^4)^2 = 4x^6$
   Ⓒ $(x^2y^{-1})^2 = \dfrac{x^4}{y^2}$
   Ⓓ $(2a^{-2})^3 = 8a^6$

CHAPTER 1 → Lesson 4: Scientific Notation

1. **In 2007, approximately 3,380,000 people visited the Statue of Liberty. Express this number in scientific notation.**

   Ⓐ 0.388×10^7
   Ⓑ 3.38×10^6
   Ⓒ 33.8×10^5
   Ⓓ 338×10^4

2. **The average distance from Saturn to the Sun is 890,800,000 miles. Express this number in scientific notation.**

   Ⓐ 8908×10^8
   Ⓑ 8908×10^5
   Ⓒ 8.908×10^8
   Ⓓ 8.908×10^5

3. **The approximate population of Los Angeles is 3.8×10^6 people. Express this number in standard notation.**

   Ⓐ 380,000
   Ⓑ 3,800,000
   Ⓒ 38,000,000
   Ⓓ 380,000,000

4. **The approximate population of Kazakhstan is 1.53×10^7 people. Express this number in standard notation.**

   Ⓐ 153,000
   Ⓑ 1,530,000
   Ⓒ 15,300,000
   Ⓓ 153,000,000

5. **The typical human body contains about 2.5×10^{-3} kilograms of zinc. Express this amount in standard form.**

   Ⓐ 0.00025 kilograms
   Ⓑ 0.0025 kilograms
   Ⓒ 0.025 kilograms
   Ⓓ 0.25 kilograms

6. If a number expressed in scientific notation is $N \times 10^5$, how large is the number?

    Ⓐ Between 1,000 (included) and 10,000
    Ⓑ Between 10,000 (included) and 100,000
    Ⓒ Between 100,000 (included) and 1,000,000
    Ⓓ Between 1,000,000 (included) and 10,000,000

7. Red light has a wavelength of 650×10^{-9} meters. Express the wavelength in scientific notation.

    Ⓐ 65.0×10^{-10} meters
    Ⓑ 65.0×10^{-8} meters
    Ⓒ 6.50×10^{-7} meters
    Ⓓ 6.50×10^{-11} meters

8. A strand of hair from a human head is approximately 1×10^{-4} meters thick. What fraction of a meter is this?

    Ⓐ $\dfrac{1}{100}$

    Ⓑ $\dfrac{1}{1,000}$

    Ⓒ $\dfrac{1}{10,000}$

    Ⓓ $\dfrac{1}{100,000}$

9. Which of the following numbers has the greatest value?

    Ⓐ 8.93×10^3
    Ⓑ 8.935×10^2
    Ⓒ 8.935×10^3
    Ⓓ 893.5×10^1

10. Which of the following numbers has the least value?

    Ⓐ -1.56×10^2
    Ⓑ -1.56×10^3
    Ⓒ 1.56×10^2
    Ⓓ 1.56×10^3

11. Which of the following are correctly written in scientific notation?

   Note that more than one option may be correct. Select all the correct options

   Ⓐ .032 x 10^5
   Ⓑ 11.002 x 10^{-1}
   Ⓒ 1.23 x 10^5
   Ⓓ 9.625 x 10^{-7}

12. Change 2,347,000,000 from standard form to scientific notation by filling in the blank boxes.

13. Convert 0.0000687 to scientific notation by filling in the blank boxes.

CHAPTER 1 → Lesson 5: Solving Problems Involving Scientific Notation

1. The population of California is approximately 3.7×10^7 people. The land area of California is approximately 1.6×10^5 square miles. Divide the population by the area to find the best estimate of the number of people per square mile in California.

   Ⓐ 24 people
   Ⓑ 240 people
   Ⓒ 2,400 people
   Ⓓ 24,000 people

2. Mercury is approximately 6×10^7 kilometers from the Sun. The speed of light is approximately 3×10^5 kilometers per second. Divide the distance by the speed of light to determine the approximate number of seconds it takes light to travel from the Sun to Mercury.

   Ⓐ 2 seconds
   Ⓑ 20 seconds
   Ⓒ 200 seconds
   Ⓓ 2,000 seconds

3. Simplify $(4 \times 10^6) \times (2 \times 10^3)$ and express the result in scientific notation.

   Ⓐ 8×10^9
   Ⓑ 8×10^{18}
   Ⓒ 6×10^9
   Ⓓ 6×10^{18}

4. Simplify $(2 \times 10^{-3}) \times (3 \times 10^5)$ and express the result in scientific notation.

   Ⓐ 5×10^{-8}
   Ⓑ 5×10^{-15}
   Ⓒ 6×10^8
   Ⓓ 6×10^2

5. Washington is approximately 2.4×10^3 miles from Utah. Mary drives 6×10^1 miles per hour from Washington to Utah. Divide the distance by the speed to determine the approximate number of hours it takes Mary to travel from Washington to Utah.

   Ⓐ 41 hours
   Ⓑ 40 hours
   Ⓒ 39 hours
   Ⓓ 38 hours

6. Which of the following is NOT equal to $(5 \times 10^5) \times (9 \times 10^{-3})$?

   Ⓐ 4.5×10^4
   Ⓑ 4.5×10^3
   Ⓒ 4,500
   Ⓓ 45×100

7. Find $(5 \times 10^7) \div (10 \times 10^2)$ and express the result in scientific notation.

   Ⓐ 5×10^4
   Ⓑ 0.5×10^5
   Ⓒ 50×10^9
   Ⓓ 5.0×10^9

8. Approximate $.00004567 \times .00001234$ and express the result in scientific notation.

   Ⓐ 5.636×10^{-8}
   Ⓑ 5.636×10^{-9}
   Ⓒ 5.636×10^{-10}
   Ⓓ None of the above.

9. Find the product $(50.67 \times 10^4) \times (12.9 \times 10^3)$ and express the answer in standard notation.

   Ⓐ 653.643
   Ⓑ 65,364,300,000
   Ⓒ 6.53643×10^9
   Ⓓ 6,536,430,000

10 Approximate the quotient and express the answer in standard notation.

   $(1.298 \times 10^4) \div (3.97 \times 10^2)$

   Ⓐ 32.7
   Ⓑ .327
   Ⓒ $.327 \times 10^2$
   Ⓓ None of the above.

11. **Which of the following examples correctly apply the rules of scientific notation? Select all the correct answers.**

   Ⓐ $(4.0 \times 10^3)(5.0 \times 10^5) = 2 \times 10^9$

   Ⓑ $\dfrac{4.5 \times 10^5}{9.0 \times 10^9} = 2 \times 10^4$

   Ⓒ $(2.1 \times 10^5) + (2.7 \times 10^5) = 4.8 \times 10^5$

   Ⓓ $(3.1 \times 10^5) - (2.7 \times 10^2) = 0.4 \times 10^3$

12. **Which of the following lists are ordered from greatest to least? Select all the correct answers.**

   Ⓐ 2.0×10^2, 3.0×10^6, 4.0×10^{-7}, 5.0×10^{12}
   Ⓑ 4.0×10^{-7}, 2.0×10^2, 3.0×10^6, 5.0×10^{12}
   Ⓒ 3.0×10^7, 3.0×10^6, 3.0×10^2, 3.0×10^{-7}
   Ⓓ 1.8×10^9, 1.5×10^6, 1.4×10^{-5}, 1.9×10^{-8}

13. $(6 \times 10^3)(9.91 \times 10^0) = $ _____

CHAPTER 1 → Lesson 6: Square & Cube Roots

1. **What is the cube root of 1,000 ?**

    Ⓐ 10

    Ⓑ 100

    Ⓒ $33\frac{1}{3}$

    Ⓓ $333\frac{1}{3}$

2. $8\sqrt{12} \div \sqrt{15} =$

    Ⓐ $\frac{4}{5}$

    Ⓑ $\frac{8}{5}$

    Ⓒ $\frac{16}{\sqrt{5}}$

    Ⓓ $\frac{\sqrt{5}}{8}$

3. **The square root of 75 is between which two integers?**

    Ⓐ 8 and 9
    Ⓑ 7 and 8
    Ⓒ 9 and 10
    Ⓓ 6 and 7

4. **The square root of 110 is between which two integers?**

    Ⓐ 10 and 11
    Ⓑ 9 and 10
    Ⓒ 11 and 12
    Ⓓ 8 and 9

5. **Solve the following problem:** $6\sqrt{20} \div \sqrt{5} =$ _____

    Ⓐ 12
    Ⓑ 11
    Ⓒ 30
    Ⓓ 5

6. The cube root of 66 is between which two integers?

Ⓐ 4 and 5
Ⓑ 3 and 4
Ⓒ 5 and 6
Ⓓ 6 and 7

7. Which expression has the same value as $3\sqrt{144} \div \sqrt{12}$?

Ⓐ $3\sqrt{12}$
Ⓑ $4\sqrt{12}$
Ⓒ $27 \div \sqrt{12}$
Ⓓ $33 \div \sqrt{12}$

8. The cubic root of 400 lies between which two numbers?

Ⓐ 5 and 6
Ⓑ 6 and 7
Ⓒ 7 and 8
Ⓓ 8 and 9

9. Which of the following is equivalent to the expression $4\sqrt{250} \div 5\sqrt{2}$?

Ⓐ $4\sqrt{25} \div 5$
Ⓑ $4\sqrt{125} \div \sqrt{2}$
Ⓒ $4\sqrt{10}$
Ⓓ $4\sqrt{5}$

10. The cube root of 150 is closest to which of the following?

Ⓐ 15
Ⓑ 10
Ⓒ 5
Ⓓ 3

11. Select all that apply: What is $\sqrt{\dfrac{81}{289}}$?

Ⓐ $\dfrac{1}{2}$

Ⓑ $\dfrac{9}{17}$

Ⓒ $\dfrac{-1}{2}$

Ⓓ $\dfrac{-9}{17}$

12. Select all the numbers which have integers as the cube roots.

Ⓐ $\sqrt[3]{27}$
Ⓑ $\sqrt[3]{9}$
Ⓒ $\sqrt[3]{1000}$
Ⓓ $\sqrt[3]{18}$

13. Fill in the boxes to make the statement true

$\sqrt[3]{8} = \boxed{}$ since $\boxed{} \times \boxed{} \times \boxed{} = 8$

End of Number Sense and Operations

Chapter 2
Algebraic Reasoning

Lesson 1: Multiplying Linear Expressions

1. **What is the result of multiplying (3x + 2) by (4x - 5)?**

   Ⓐ $12x^2 - 13x - 10$
   Ⓑ $12x^2 - x - 10$
   Ⓒ $12x^2 + x - 10$
   Ⓓ $12x^2 - 13x + 10$

2. **Simplify $(\frac{2}{3}) \times (6x - 9)$.**

   Ⓐ $12x^2 - 13x - 10$
   Ⓑ $12x^2 - x - 10$
   Ⓒ $12x^2 + x - 10$
   Ⓓ $12x^2 - 13x + 10$

3. **What is the product of $(-\frac{5}{6})x$ and (12x + 18)?**

   Ⓐ $-10x^2 + 3x$
   Ⓑ $-10x^2 - 15x$
   Ⓒ $10x^2 + 3x$
   Ⓓ $10x^2 - 3x$

4. **Simplify $(\frac{4}{5})(2x^2 - 10x)$.**

   Ⓐ $8x^2 - 40x$
   Ⓑ $8x^2 + 40x$
   Ⓒ $\frac{8}{5}x^2 - 8x$
   Ⓓ $8x^2 + 20x$

5. **Multiply (3x - 4) by (2x + 5).**

   Ⓐ $-6x^2 - 7x - 20$
   Ⓑ $6x^2 - 7x + 20$
   Ⓒ $6x^2 + 7x - 20$
   Ⓓ $6x^2 + 7x + 20$

6. **What is the product of ($-\frac{1}{2}$)x and (-6x - 8)?**

    Ⓐ $3x^2 + 4x$
    Ⓑ $-3x^2 + 4x$
    Ⓒ $3x^2 - 4x$
    Ⓓ $-3x^2 - 4x$

7. **Simplify ($\frac{5}{7}$)(-7x² + 14x).**

    Ⓐ $-5x^2 + 10x$
    Ⓑ $5x^2 - 10x$
    Ⓒ $-5x^2 - 10x$
    Ⓓ $5x^2 + 10x$

8. **Multiply (2x - 3) by (3x + 4).**

    Ⓐ $6x^2 + 5x - 12$
    Ⓑ $6x^2 + 5x + 12$
    Ⓒ $6x^2 - x - 12$
    Ⓓ $6x^2 - 5x + 12$

9. **What is the product of ($\frac{1}{4}$)x and (8x - 16)?**

    Ⓐ $2x^2 - 4x$
    Ⓑ $2x^2 + 4x$
    Ⓒ $8x^2 - 16x$
    Ⓓ $8x^2 + 16x$

10. **Simplify (-3x+5)(-10x² + 15x).**

    Ⓐ $30x^3 - 65x^2 + 75x$
    Ⓑ $-6x^2 + 9x$
    Ⓒ $6x^2 + 9x$
    Ⓓ $-6x^2 - 9x$

Date of Completion:_____   Score:_____

CHAPTER 2 → Lesson 2: Factorizing Algebraic Expressions

1. **Rewrite 3x + 6y as a common factor multiplied by the sum of two algebraic expressions.**

   Ⓐ 3(x + y)
   Ⓑ 3x(1 + 2y)
   Ⓒ 3(x + 2y)
   Ⓓ 3x + 6y

2. **Express 4a² + 8ab as a common factor multiplied by the sum of two algebraic expressions.**

   Ⓐ 4a(a + 2b)
   Ⓑ 4a²(b + 2)
   Ⓒ 4a(a + 4b)
   Ⓓ 4(a² + 2ab)

3. **Rewrite 5xy + 10yz as a common factor multiplied by the sum of two algebraic expressions.**

   Ⓐ 5(x + 2y)
   Ⓑ 5y(x + 2z)
   Ⓒ 5(xy + 2yz)
   Ⓓ 5y(x + 10z)

4. **Express 6m³ + 12m²n as a common factor multiplied by the sum of two algebraic expressions.**

   Ⓐ 6m(m² + 2mn)
   Ⓑ 6m²(m + 2n)
   Ⓒ 6m(m² + 2m²n)
   Ⓓ 6m(m³ + 2m²n)

5. **Rewrite 7a²b - 14ab² as a common factor multiplied by the sum of two algebraic expressions.**

   Ⓐ 7ab(a - 2b)
   Ⓑ 7ab(1 - 2b)
   Ⓒ 7a(a - 2b)
   Ⓓ 7(a²b - 2ab²)

6. **Express 8x² + 16xy + 24xz as a common factor multiplied by the sum of two algebraic expressions.**

   Ⓐ 8x(1 + 2y + 3z)
   Ⓑ 8x(x + 2y + 3z)
   Ⓒ 8x²(1 + 2y + 3z)
   Ⓓ 8(x² + 2xy + 3xz)

7. Rewrite $9ab^2 + 18bc^2$ as a common factor multiplied by the sum of two algebraic expressions.

    Ⓐ $9b(ab + 2c^2)$
    Ⓑ $9b^2(a + 2c^2)$
    Ⓒ $9b(a + 6c)$
    Ⓓ $9(b^2 + 2bc^2)$

8. Express $10x^3 + 20x^2y - 30xy^2$ as a common factor multiplied by the sum of two algebraic expressions.

    Ⓐ $10x^2(x + 2y - 3y^2)$
    Ⓑ $10x(x^2 + 2xy - 3y^2)$
    Ⓒ $10x^2(x + 2y + 3y^2)$
    Ⓓ $10x(x^2 + 2xy + 3y^2)$

9. Rewrite $11a^2b^3 + 22a^2bc^2$ as a common factor multiplied by the sum of two algebraic expressions.

    Ⓐ $11a^2b(b^2 + 2c^2)$
    Ⓑ $11a^2b^2(b + 2c^2)$
    Ⓒ $11a^2b(b^2 + 2c)$
    Ⓓ $11(a^2b^3 + 2a^2bc^2)$

10. Factor out the common monomial for: $12xy^2z + 24xyz^2$

    Ⓐ $12xyz(y + 2z)$
    Ⓑ $12xyz^2(y + 2z)$
    Ⓒ $12xyz(y^2 + 2z)$
    Ⓓ $12(xy^2z + 2xyz^2)$

CHAPTER 2 → Lesson 3: Solving Linear Equations

1. Which two consecutive odd integers have a sum of 44?

   Ⓐ 21 and 23
   Ⓑ 19 and 21
   Ⓒ 23 and 25
   Ⓓ 17 and 19

2. During each of the first three quarters of the school year, Melissa earned a grade point average of 2.1, 2.9, and 3.1. What does her 4th quarter grade point average need to be in order to raise her grade to a 3.0 cumulative grade point average?

   Ⓐ 3.9
   Ⓑ 4.2
   Ⓒ 2.6
   Ⓓ 3.5

3. Martha is on a trip of 1,924 miles. She has already traveled 490 miles. She has 3 days left on her trip. How many miles does she need to travel each day to complete her trip?

   Ⓐ 450 miles/day
   Ⓑ 464 miles/day
   Ⓒ 478 miles/day
   Ⓓ 492 miles/day

4. Find the solution to the following equation: $3x + 5 = 29$

   Ⓐ $x = 24$
   Ⓑ $x = 11$
   Ⓒ $x = 8$
   Ⓓ $x = 6$

5. Find the solution to the following equation:
   $7 - 2x = 13 - 2x$

   Ⓐ $x = -10$
   Ⓑ $x = -3$
   Ⓒ $x = 3$
   Ⓓ There is no solution.

6. Find the solution to the following equation: 6x + 1 = 4x - 3

   Ⓐ x = -1
   Ⓑ x = -2
   Ⓒ x = - 0.5
   Ⓓ There is no solution.

7. Find the solution to the following equation:
   2x + 6 + 1 = 7 + 2x

   Ⓐ x = -3
   Ⓑ x = 3
   Ⓒ x = 7
   Ⓓ All real numbers are solutions.

8. Find the solution to the following equation: 8x-1=8x

   Ⓐ x = 7
   Ⓑ x = -8
   Ⓒ x = 8
   Ⓓ There is no solution.

9. Which of the answers is the correct solution to the following equation?
   2x + 5x - 9 = 8x - x - 3 - 6

   Ⓐ x = 3
   Ⓑ x = 7
   Ⓒ x = 9
   Ⓓ All real values for x are correct solutions.

10. Solve the following linear equation for y.
    -y + 7y -54 = 0

   Ⓐ y = 0
   Ⓑ y = 1
   Ⓒ y = 6
   Ⓓ y = 9

11. Solve each equation for the variable. Select the ones whose values of the variables are the same.

    Note that more than one option may be correct. Select all the correct answers.

    Ⓐ -5m = 25
    Ⓑ -10c = -80
    Ⓒ -7 + g = -12
    Ⓓ 12m + 20 = -40

12. Solve for x: 5x + 20 = -20.

    x = ?

    Write your answer in the box given below.

13. Fill in the missing number to make this equation true, if x = -3.

    7+3x=5x+_____

CHAPTER 2 → Lesson 4: Solve Linear Equations with Rational Numbers

1. Solve the following linear equation: $\dfrac{7}{14} = n + \dfrac{7}{14}n$

   Ⓐ $n = 1\dfrac{1}{2}$

   Ⓑ $n = 3$

   Ⓒ $n = \dfrac{1}{3}$

   Ⓓ $n = 1$

2. Find the solution to the following equation: $2(2x - 7) = 14$

   Ⓐ $x = 14$
   Ⓑ $x = 7$
   Ⓒ $x = 1$
   Ⓓ $x = 0$

3. Solve the following equation for x.
   $6x - (2x + 5) = 11$

   Ⓐ $x = -3$
   Ⓑ $x = -4$
   Ⓒ $x = 3$
   Ⓓ $x = 4$

4. $4x + 2(x - 3) = 0$

   Ⓐ $x = 0$
   Ⓑ $x = 1$
   Ⓒ $x = 2$
   Ⓓ All real values for x are correct solutions.

5. Solve the following equation for y.
   $3y - 7(y + 5) = y - 35$

   Ⓐ $y = 0$
   Ⓑ $y = 1$
   Ⓒ $y = 2$
   Ⓓ All real values for y are correct solutions.

6. Solve the following linear equation: $2(x-5) = \frac{1}{2}(6x+4)$

   Ⓐ x= -12
   Ⓑ x= -9
   Ⓒ x= -4
   Ⓓ There is no solution.

7. Solve the following linear equation for x.

   $3x + 2 + x = \frac{1}{3}(12x + 6)$

   Ⓐ x= -4
   Ⓑ x= 2
   Ⓒ There is no solution.
   Ⓓ All real values for x are correct solutions.

8. $\frac{1}{2}x + \frac{2}{3}x + 5 = \frac{5}{2}x + 6$

   Ⓐ $x = \frac{33}{4}$

   Ⓑ $x = \frac{1}{2}$

   Ⓒ $x = -\frac{3}{4}$

   Ⓓ $x = -\frac{6}{5}$

9. Which of the following could be a correct procedure for solving the equation below?
   $2(2x+3) = 3(2x+5)$

   Ⓐ 4x+5 = 6x+5
      -2x+5 = 5
      -2x = 0
      x = 0

   Ⓒ 2(5x) = 6x+15
      10x = 6x+15
      4x = 15

      $x = \frac{15}{4}$

   Ⓑ 4x+6 = 6x+15
      -2x+6 = 15
      -2x = 9

      $x = -\frac{9}{2}$

   Ⓓ 4x+6 = 6x+15
      -2x+6 = 15
      -2x = 9

      $x = \frac{2}{9}$

10. Solve the following linear equation:
    $0.64x - 0.15x + 0.08 = 0.09x$

    Ⓐ $x = -5$
    Ⓑ $x = -0.2$
    Ⓒ $x = 5.125$
    Ⓓ There is no solution.

11. Which of the following statements are true? Select all that apply.

    Ⓐ $w - \dfrac{2}{5} = \dfrac{8}{5}$ so $w=2$

    Ⓑ $\dfrac{-5}{8} y = 15$ so $y=24$

    Ⓒ $0.4x - 1.2 = 0.15x + 0.8$ so $x=8$

    Ⓓ $\dfrac{x}{6} = -5$ so $x=30$

12. Select the answer choice with the correct order of how you would solve the equation.

    $$\dfrac{3}{4} + \dfrac{1}{2}\left(m + \dfrac{1}{4}\right) = \dfrac{19}{16}$$

    A --> $m = \dfrac{5}{8}$ B --> $\dfrac{1}{2}\left(m + \dfrac{1}{4}\right) = \dfrac{7}{16}$ C --> $\left(m + \dfrac{1}{4}\right) = \dfrac{7}{8}$

    Ⓐ A B C
    Ⓑ B C A
    Ⓒ C A B

13. Solve the following linear equation:

    $$\dfrac{8}{16} = n + \dfrac{8}{16} n$$

CHAPTER 2 → Lesson 5: Two-step Linear Inequalities

1. **Solve the inequality: 3x + 5 > 11.**

   Ⓐ x < 2
   Ⓑ x > 2
   Ⓒ x < 6
   Ⓓ x > 6

2. **Solve the inequality: 2x - 4 ≤ 10.**

   Ⓐ x ≤ 7
   Ⓑ x ≤ 8
   Ⓒ x ≥ 7
   Ⓓ x ≥ 8

3. **Solve the inequality: -5x + 8 > 3x - 6.**

   Ⓐ $x > \dfrac{7}{4}$

   Ⓑ x < 2

   Ⓒ $x > \dfrac{7}{4}$

   Ⓓ $x < \dfrac{7}{4}$

4. **Solve the inequality: 4(2x + 1) ≤ 12.**

   Ⓐ x ≤ 0
   Ⓑ x ≥ 0
   Ⓒ x ≤ 1
   Ⓓ x ≥ 1

5. **Solve the inequality: -3(2x - 1) > 5x + 2.**

   Ⓐ $x < -\dfrac{1}{2}$

   Ⓑ $x > -\dfrac{1}{2}$

   Ⓒ $x < \dfrac{1}{11}$

   Ⓓ $x > \dfrac{1}{2}$

6. **Solve the inequality: 2(x - 3) + 7 ≥ 13.**

    Ⓐ x ≥ 6
    Ⓑ x ≤ 5
    Ⓒ x ≥ 3
    Ⓓ x ≤ 3

7. **Solve the inequality: -2(x + 4) < 6x - 5.**

    Ⓐ x < 1

    Ⓑ x > $\frac{1}{3}$

    Ⓒ x < -$\frac{3}{8}$

    Ⓓ x > -$\frac{1}{8}$

8. **Solve the inequality: 3(2x + 3) - 4 ≤ 5(x - 1).**

    Ⓐ x ≤ -10

    Ⓑ x ≥ -1

    Ⓒ x ≤ $\frac{7}{4}$

    Ⓓ x ≥ $\frac{7}{4}$

9. **Solve the inequality: 2x + 3 < 3x - 1.**

    Ⓐ x > 4
    Ⓑ x < 4
    Ⓒ x < -4
    Ⓓ x > -4

10. **Solve the inequality: 5 - 2x ≥ 3x + 7.**

    Ⓐ x ≤ $\frac{2}{5}$

    Ⓑ b) x ≥ -4
    Ⓒ c) x ≤ 4
    Ⓓ d) x ≥ 4

CHAPTER 2 → Lesson 6: Proportional Relationships

1. **Suppose you have a set of data points (x, y) given by:**
   (1, 3), (2, 6), (3, 9), (4, 12), (5, 15)
   Is the relationship between x and y linear and proportional?

   Ⓐ Yes
   Ⓑ No

2. **Consider the data points (x, y) shown below:**
   (2, 5), (4, 10), (6, 15), (8, 21), (10, 25)
   Is the relationship between x and y linear and proportional?

   Ⓐ Yes
   Ⓑ No

3. **Examine the data points (x, y) given below:**
   (3, 6), (5, 10), (7, 14), (9, 18), (11, 22)
   Is the relationship between x and y linear and proportional?

   Ⓐ Yes
   Ⓑ No

4. **Given the following data points, determine if the relationship is both linear and proportional:**

x	y
1	3
2	6
3	9
4	12

   Ⓐ Yes
   Ⓑ No

5. Examine the data below and determine if the relationship is linear and proportional:

x	y
2	5
4	10
6	15
8	20

Ⓐ Yes
Ⓑ No

6. Investigate the data provided and ascertain if the relationship is linear and proportional:

x	y
2	4
3	7
4	10
5	13

Ⓐ Yes
Ⓑ No

7. When plotting a graph of a proportional relationship, what does the line passing through the origin represent?

Ⓐ The y-intercept
Ⓑ The slope of the line
Ⓒ The proportionality constant
Ⓓ The x-intercept

8. In a proportional relationship, what is the graph of y as a function of x?

Ⓐ A straight line passing through the origin
Ⓑ A parabola
Ⓒ An exponential curve
Ⓓ A circle

9. If the relationship between x and y is proportional, what is the equation that represents this relationship?

    Ⓐ y = mx + b
    Ⓑ y = ax² + bx + c
    Ⓒ y = kx
    Ⓓ y = eˣ

10. If the graph of a relationship between x and y is a horizontal line, is the relationship proportional?

    Ⓐ Yes
    Ⓑ No

CHAPTER 2 → Lesson 7: Compare Proportions

1. Find the unit rate if 12 tablets cost $1,440.

    Ⓐ $100
    Ⓑ $150
    Ⓒ $120
    Ⓓ $50

2. A package of Big Bubbles Gum has 10 pieces and sells for $2.90. A package of Fruity Gum has 20 pieces and sells for $6.20. Compare the unit prices.

    Ⓐ Big Bubbles is $0.10 more per piece than Fruity.
    Ⓑ Fruity is $0.02 more per piece than Big Bubbles.
    Ⓒ They both have the same unit price.
    Ⓓ It cannot be determined.

3. The first major ski slope in Vermont has a rise of 9 feet vertically for every 54 feet horizontally. A second ski slope has a rise of 12 feet vertically for every 84 feet horizontally. Which of the following statements is true?

    Ⓐ The first slope is steeper than the second.
    Ⓑ The second slope is steeper than the first.
    Ⓒ Both slopes have the same steepness.
    Ⓓ Cannot be determined from the information given.

4. Which of the following ramps has the steepest slope?

    Ⓐ Ramp A has a vertical rise of 3 feet and a horizontal run of 15 feet
    Ⓑ Ramp B has a vertical rise of 4 feet and a horizontal run of 12 feet
    Ⓒ Ramp C has a vertical rise of 2 feet and a horizontal run of 10 feet
    Ⓓ Ramp D has a vertical rise of 5 feet and a horizontal run of 20 feet

5. Choose the statement that is true about unit rate.

    Ⓐ The unit rate can also be called the rate of change.
    Ⓑ The unit rate can also be called the mode.
    Ⓒ The unit rate can also be called the frequency.
    Ⓓ The unit rate can also be called the median.

6. Which statement is false?

Ⓐ Unit cost is calculated by dividing the amount of items by the total cost.
Ⓑ Unit cost is calculated by dividing the total cost by the amount of items.
Ⓒ Unit cost is the cost of one unit item.
Ⓓ On similar items, a higher unit cost is not the better price.

7. Selena is preparing for her eighth grade graduation party. She must keep within the budget set by her parents. Which is the best price for her to purchase ice cream?

Ⓐ $3.99/ 24 oz carton
Ⓑ $4.80/ one-quart carton
Ⓒ $11.00 / one gallon tub
Ⓓ $49.60/ five gallon tub

8. Ben is building a ramp for his skate boarding club. Which of the following provides the least steep ramp?

Ⓐ 2 feet vertical for every 10 feet horizontal
Ⓑ 3 feet vertical for every 9 feet horizontal
Ⓒ 4 feet vertical for every 16 feet horizontal
Ⓓ 5 feet vertical for every 30 feet horizontal

9. Riley is shopping for tee shirts. Which is the most expensive (based on unit price per shirt)?

Ⓐ 5 tee shirts for $50.00
Ⓑ 6 tee shirts for $90.00
Ⓒ 2 tee shirts for $22.00
Ⓓ 4 tee shirts for $48.00

10. The swim team is preparing for a meet. Which of the following is Lindy's fastest time?

Ⓐ five laps in fifteen minutes
Ⓑ four laps in sixteen minutes
Ⓒ two laps in ten minutes
Ⓓ three laps in eighteen minutes

11. David is having a Super Bowl party and he needs bottled sodas. Which of the following purchases will give him the lowest unit cost?

Ⓐ $2.00 for a 6 pack
Ⓑ $6.00 for a 24 pack
Ⓒ $3.60 for a 12 pack
Ⓓ $10.00 for a 36 pack

12. A package of plain wafers has 20 per pack and sells for $2.40. A package of sugar-free wafers has 30 pieces and sells for $6.30. Compare the unit prices.

Ⓐ Each plain wafer is $0.17 more than a sugar-free wafer.
Ⓑ Each sugar-free wafer is $0.09 more than a plain wafer.
Ⓒ They both have the same unit price per wafer.
Ⓓ The relationship cannot be determined.

13. Li took 4 practice tests to prepare for his chapter test.
Which of the following is the best score?

Ⓐ 36 correct out of 40 questions
Ⓑ 24 correct out of 30 questions
Ⓒ 17 correct out of 25 questions
Ⓓ 15 correct out of 20 questions

14. Mel's class is planning a fundraiser. They have decided to have a carnival. If they sell tickets in packs of 40 for $30.00, what is the unit cost?

Ⓐ $4.00 per ticket
Ⓑ $0.50 per ticket
Ⓒ $1.75 per ticket
Ⓓ $0.75 per ticket

15. Which of the following ski slopes has the steepest slope?

Ⓐ Ski Slope A has a vertical rise of 4 feet and a horizontal run of 16 feet
Ⓑ Ski Slope B has a vertical rise of 3 feet and a horizontal run of 12 feet
Ⓒ Ski Slope C has a vertical rise of 3 feet and a horizontal run of 9 feet
Ⓓ Ski Slope D has a vertical rise of 5 feet and a horizontal run of 25 feet

16. Solve for the proportion for the missing number.

$$\frac{2}{7} = \frac{4}{\boxed{}}$$

Fill in the blank box with the correct answer.

17. Solve for the proportion for the missing number.

$$\frac{20}{\boxed{}} = \frac{16}{20}$$

Fill in the blank box with the correct answer.

18. Write a proportion to solve this word problem. Then solve the proportion.

Kasey bought 32 kiwi fruit for $16. How many kiwi can Lisa buy if she has $4?

CHAPTER 2 → Lesson 8: Understanding Slope

1. **Which of the following statements is true about slope?**

   Ⓐ Slopes of straight lines will always be positive numbers.
   Ⓑ The slopes vary between the points on a straight line.
   Ⓒ Slope is determined by dividing the horizontal distance between two points by the corresponding vertical distance.
   Ⓓ Slope is determined by dividing the vertical distance between two points by the corresponding horizontal distance.

2. **Which of the following is an equation of the line passing through the points (-1, 4) and (1, 2)?**

   Ⓐ $y = x - 3$
   Ⓑ $y = 2x + 2$
   Ⓒ $y = -2x + 4$
   Ⓓ $y = -x + 3$

3. **The graph of which equation has the same slope as the graph of $y = 4x + 3$?**

   Ⓐ $y = -2x + 3$
   Ⓑ $y = 2x - 3$
   Ⓒ $y = -4x + 2$
   Ⓓ $y = 4x - 2$

4. **Which of these lines has the greatest slope?**

   Ⓐ $y = \frac{8}{5}x - 7$

   Ⓑ $y = \frac{6}{5}x + 4$

   Ⓒ $y = \frac{7}{5}x + 2$

   Ⓓ $y = \frac{9}{5}x - 3$

5. **Which of these lines has the smallest slope?**

   Ⓐ $y = \frac{1}{8}x + 7$

   Ⓑ $y = \frac{1}{3}x + 7$

   Ⓒ $y = \frac{1}{4}x - 9$

   Ⓓ $y = \frac{1}{7}x$

6. Fill in the blank with one of the four choices to make the following a true statement. Knowing _____ and the y-intercept is **NOT** enough for us to write the equation of the line.

Ⓐ direction
Ⓑ a point on a given line
Ⓒ the x-intercept
Ⓓ the slope

7. A skateboarder is practicing at the city park. He is skating up and down the steepest straight line ramp. If the highest point on the ramp is 30 feet above the ground and the horizontal distance from the base of the ramp to a point directly beneath the upper end is 500 feet, what is the slope of the ramp?

Ⓐ $\dfrac{500}{30}$

Ⓑ $\dfrac{50}{3}$

Ⓒ $\dfrac{3}{50}$

Ⓓ None of these.

8. If the equation of a line is expressed as $y = \dfrac{3}{2}x - 9$, what is the slope of the line?

Ⓐ - 9

Ⓑ +9

Ⓒ $\dfrac{3}{2}$

Ⓓ $\dfrac{2}{3}$

9. Which of the following is an equation of the line that passes through the points (0, 5) and (2, 15)?

Ⓐ y = 5x + 5
Ⓑ y = 5x + 3
Ⓒ y = 3x + 5
Ⓓ y = 5x - 5

10. Which of the following equations has the same slope as the line passing through the points (1, 6) and (3, 10)?

  Ⓐ y = 2x - 9
  Ⓑ y = 5x - 2
  Ⓒ y = 4x - 5
  Ⓓ y = 9x - 6

11. Which of the following equations has the same slope as the line passing through the points (3, 6) and (5, 10)?

  Ⓐ y = 2x -12
  Ⓑ y = 11x - 8
  Ⓒ y = -2x - 9
  Ⓓ y = 3x - 5

12. Which equation has the same slope as y = -5x - 4?

  Ⓐ y = 5x +15
  Ⓑ y = -5x - 11
  Ⓒ y = 5x -19
  Ⓓ y = 5x - 13

13. Find the slope of the line passing through the points (3,3) and (5,5).

  Ⓐ 2
  Ⓑ 1
  Ⓒ 3
  Ⓓ 5

14. Which of the following lines has the steepest slope?

  Ⓐ y = 4x+5
  Ⓑ y =-3x + 5
  Ⓒ y = 3x - 5
  Ⓓ They all have the same slope.

15. Which of the following is the equation of the line passing through the points (0,-3) and (-3,0) ?

  Ⓐ y = -3x + 3
  Ⓑ y = -3x
  Ⓒ y = -x - 3
  Ⓓ y = -x

16. Find the slope between the points (-12, -5) and (0, 8).

    Write your answer in the box given below.

17. Find the slope between the points (3, -3) and (12, -2).

    Write your answer in the box given below.

18. Find the slope between the points (1, 2) and (5, -7).

    Write your answer in the box given below.

CHAPTER 2 → Lesson 9: Expressing Linear Equations

1. The cost of renting a bicycle is $5 for the first hour and $2 for each additional hour. Write the equation that represents the cost (C) in terms of the number of hours (h) the bicycle is rented.

   Ⓐ C = 2h + 3
   Ⓑ C = 5h + 2
   Ⓒ C = 2h - 5
   Ⓓ C = 5h - 2

2. A car rental company charges a flat fee of $30 per day plus an additional $0.15 per mile driven. Write the equation that represents the total cost (C) in terms of the number of miles driven (m).

   Ⓐ C = 0.15m + 30
   Ⓑ C = 30m + 0.15
   Ⓒ C = 0.15m - 30
   Ⓓ C = 30 - 0.15m

3. A line passes through the points (2, 5) and (4, 9). What is the equation of the line in slope-intercept form?

   Ⓐ y = 2x + 1
   Ⓑ y = 2x + 3
   Ⓒ y = 4x + 1
   Ⓓ y = 4x + 3

4. The temperature in Celsius can be converted to Fahrenheit using the equation F = 1.8C + 32. What is the Fahrenheit temperature equivalent to 25°C?

   Ⓐ 57°F
   Ⓑ 77°F
   Ⓒ 47°F
   Ⓓ 67°F

5. A garden store sells plants for $10 each. Let's denote the number of plants as "n" and the total cost as "C". Which equation represents the relationship between the number of plants and the total cost?

   Ⓐ n = C + 10
   Ⓑ C = 10n
   Ⓒ n = 10C
   Ⓓ C = n + 10

6. The height (h) of a plant in inches is directly proportional to the number of days (d) since it was planted. After 10 days, the plant is 25 inches tall. Write the equation that represents this relationship.

   Ⓐ h = 10d + 25
   Ⓑ h = 2.5d
   Ⓒ h = d + 10 + 25
   Ⓓ h = 10 + 25d

7. A company offers a cell phone plan with a $20 monthly fee and $0.05 per text message sent. Write the equation for the total cost (C) based on the number of text messages sent (t) in a month.

   Ⓐ C = 0.05t + 20
   Ⓑ C = 20t + 0.05
   Ⓒ C = 20 + 0.05t
   Ⓓ C = 0.05 + 20t

8. The cost C (in dollars) to rent a car for d days is given by the equation C=25+40d. What does the slope of this equation represent?

   Ⓐ The initial cost of renting the car.
   Ⓑ The cost per day to rent the car.
   Ⓒ The total cost of renting the car.
   Ⓓ The number of days the car has been rented.

9. The equation y=−2x+7 represents a line in a coordinate system. What is the slope of this line?

   Ⓐ 2
   Ⓑ -2
   Ⓒ 7
   Ⓓ -7

10. You are conducting an experiment where you measure the time (t) it takes for a pendulum to complete one full swing based on its length (L). You find that the relationship between t and L is given by t=2L+1. What does the slope of this equation represent?

   Ⓐ The rate of change of the time (t) with respect to the length of the pendulum.
   Ⓑ The period of the pendulum.
   Ⓒ The time it takes for two pendulum swings.
   Ⓓ The initial time when the pendulum is released.

CHAPTER 2 → Lesson 10: Interpreting Slope

1. **Suppose an equation is given as y = 2x + 5. What does the slope represent in this context?**

   Ⓐ The initial value
   Ⓑ The rate of change
   Ⓒ The y-intercept
   Ⓓ The x-intercept

2. **If a linear equation is given as d = -0.3t + 50, where d represents distance and t represents time, what does the y-intercept represent?**

   Ⓐ The initial distance
   Ⓑ The rate of change of distance
   Ⓒ The initial time
   Ⓓ The rate of change of time

3. **Given the equation V = 0.8t - 2.5, where V is voltage and t is time, what does the slope indicate?**

   Ⓐ The initial voltage
   Ⓑ The rate of change of voltage
   Ⓒ The initial time
   Ⓓ The rate of change of time

4. **If the equation of a line is given as p = -0.5t + 20, where p is population and t is time, what does the y-intercept signify?**

   Ⓐ The initial population
   Ⓑ The rate of change of population
   Ⓒ The initial time
   Ⓓ The rate of change of time

5. **Suppose the equation y = 3x - 10 represents a certain situation. What does the slope represent in this context?**

   Ⓐ The starting point
   Ⓑ The rate of change
   Ⓒ The y-intercept
   Ⓓ The growth factor

6. Given the equation w = 2.5t + 15, where w is weight and t is time, what does the slope indicate?

   Ⓐ The starting weight
   Ⓑ The rate of change of weight
   Ⓒ The initial time
   Ⓓ The rate of change of time

7. Suppose the equation n = -0.6t + 30 relates n to t. What does the y-intercept signify?

   Ⓐ The initial value of n
   Ⓑ B) The rate of change of n
   Ⓒ C) The initial time
   Ⓓ D) The rate of change of time

8. Given the equation s = 1.2t - 5, where s is distance and t is time, what does the slope indicate?

   Ⓐ The starting distance
   Ⓑ The rate of change of distance
   Ⓒ The initial time
   Ⓓ The rate of change of time

9. Suppose the equation N = -0.5t + 25 describes a situation. What does the y-intercept represent?

   Ⓐ The initial value of N
   Ⓑ B) The rate of change of N
   Ⓒ C) The initial time
   Ⓓ D) The rate of change of time

10. If the equation f = 2t + 10 represents a situation, what does the slope indicate?

   Ⓐ The starting value
   Ⓑ The rate of change
   Ⓒ The y-intercept
   Ⓓ The growth factor

CHAPTER 2 → Lesson 11: Solving Systems of Equations

1. Find the solution to the following system of equations:
   $13x + 3y = 15$ and $y = 5 - 4x$.

   Ⓐ $x = 0, y = 5$
   Ⓑ $x = 5, y = 0$
   Ⓒ $x = 9, y = -31$
   Ⓓ All real numbers are solutions.

2. Solve the system:
   $y = 2x + 5$
   $y = 3x - 7$

   Ⓐ $x = 12, y = 29$
   Ⓑ $x = 3, y = 11$
   Ⓒ $x = 5, y = -2$
   Ⓓ $x = -1, y = 3$

3. Solve the system:
   $2x + 3y = 14$
   $2x - 3y = -10$

   Ⓐ $x = 1, y = 4$
   Ⓑ $x = 2, y = 12$
   Ⓒ $x = 4, y = 2$
   Ⓓ $x = 10, y = 10$

4. Solve the system:
   $x = 13 + 2y$
   $x - 2y = 13$

   Ⓐ $x = 0, y = 13$
   Ⓑ $x = 13, y = 0$
   Ⓒ There is no solution.
   Ⓓ There are infinitely many solutions.

5. Solve the system:
   $2x + 5y = 12$
   $2x + 5y = 9$

   Ⓐ $x = 1, y = 2$
   Ⓑ $x = 2, y = 1$
   Ⓒ There is no solution.
   Ⓓ There are infinitely many solutions.

6. Solve the system:
-4x + 7y = 26
4x + 7y = 2

   Ⓐ x = -3, y = 2
   Ⓑ x = 3, y = -2
   Ⓒ x = -2, y = 3
   Ⓓ x = 2, y = -3

7. Find the solution to the following system:
y + 3x = 11
y - 2x = 1

   Ⓐ x = -5, y = 2
   Ⓑ x = 2, y = 5
   Ⓒ x = -2, y = -5
   Ⓓ x = -2, y = 5

8. Solve the system:
2x + 4y = 14
x + 2y = 7

   Ⓐ x = -1, y = 4
   Ⓑ x = 1, y = 3
   Ⓒ There is no solution.
   Ⓓ There are infinitely many solutions.

9. Solve the system:
3(y - 2x) = 9
x - 4 = 0

   Ⓐ x = -4, y = -5
   Ⓑ x = 4, y = 11
   Ⓒ There is no solution.
   Ⓓ There are infinitely many solutions.

10. Solve the system:

$10x = -5(y+2)$

$y = 3x-7$

Ⓐ $x = -1, y = 4$

Ⓑ $x = 2, y = 2$

Ⓒ $x = 2, y = -2$

Ⓓ $x = 1, y = -4$

11. Which of these will have one solution?

Note that more than one option may be correct. Select all the correct answers.

Ⓐ $y = \dfrac{3}{4}x + 1$

$y = -\dfrac{1}{2}x - 4$

Ⓑ $y = -3x + 2$

$3x + y = -4$

Ⓒ $y = \dfrac{1}{3}x - 3$

$2x + y = 4$

Ⓓ $-x + 2y = -2$

$4y = 2x - 4$

12. Fill in the table with correct solution for each system of equations.

SYSTEM	SOLUTION
$y = \dfrac{1}{2}x - 1$ $y = -\dfrac{1}{4}x - 4$	
$y = 2x + 4$ $y = -3x - 1$	
$y = 4$ $y = 7x - 3$	
$y = -\dfrac{2}{3}x - 4$ $y = \dfrac{5}{3}x + 3$	

13. Select the systems that have no solution.

Note that more than one option may be correct. Select all the correct answers.

(A) $\begin{array}{l} y= -4x+7 \\ y=-3x+3 \end{array}$

(B) $\begin{array}{l} y=\dfrac{3}{4}x-3 \\ y=\dfrac{3}{4}x+2 \end{array}$

(C) $\begin{array}{l} y= x-2 \\ y=x+2 \end{array}$

(D) $\begin{array}{l} y=2x+3 \\ 4x-2y=8 \end{array}$

(E) $\begin{array}{l} y+2x=-12 \\ y=x+15 \end{array}$

14. Fill in the table with correct solution for each system of equations.

SYSTEM	NUMBER OF SOLUTIONS
$\begin{cases} -x + 2y = 14 \\ x - 2y = -11 \end{cases}$	
$\begin{cases} 2x + 5y = 5 \\ -2x - y = -23 \end{cases}$	
$\begin{cases} y = 3x + 6 \\ -6x+2y =12 \end{cases}$	

CHAPTER 2 → Lesson 12: Solutions to Systems of Equations

1. Which of the following points is the intersection of the graphs of the lines given by the equations y = x - 5 and y = 2x + 1 ?

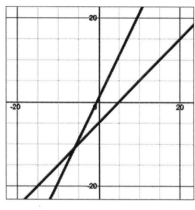

   Ⓐ (1, 3)
   Ⓑ (-1, -4)
   Ⓒ (-2, -3)
   Ⓓ (-6, -11)

2. Which of the following describes the solution set of this system?
   y = 0.5x + 7
   y = 0.5x - 1

   Ⓐ The solution is (-2, -3) because the graphs of the two equations intersect at that point.
   Ⓑ The solution is (0.5, 3) because the graphs of the two equations intersect at that point.
   Ⓒ There is no solution because the graphs of the two equations are parallel lines.
   Ⓓ There are infinitely many solutions because the graphs of the two equations are the same line.

3. Find the solution to the following system:
   y = 2(2 - 3x)
   y = -3(2x + 3)

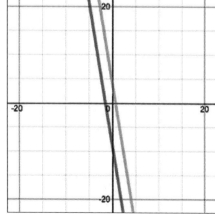

   Ⓐ x = -1; y = 10
   Ⓑ x = -2; y = 24
   Ⓒ x = -3; y = 22
   Ⓓ There is no solution.

 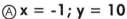

4. Use the graph, to find the solution to the following system:

$$\frac{x}{2} + \frac{y}{3} = 2$$

$$3x - 2y = 48$$

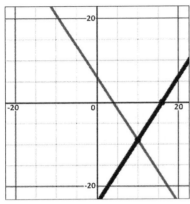

Ⓐ x = 8, y = -6
Ⓑ x = 10, y = -9
Ⓒ x = 12, y = -3
Ⓓ x = 16, y = 0

5. Which of the following best describes the relationship between the graphs of the equations in this system?

y = 2x - 6
y = -2x + 6

Ⓐ The lines intersect at the point (0, -3).
Ⓑ The lines intersect at the point (3, 0).
Ⓒ The lines do not intersect because their slopes are opposites and their y-intercepts are opposites.
Ⓓ They are the same line because their slopes are opposites and their y-intercepts are opposites.

6. Solve the system:

   $2x + 3y = 14$
   $2x - 3y = -10$

   Ⓐ $x = 1, y = 4$
   Ⓑ $x = 2, y = 12$
   Ⓒ $x = 4, y = 2$
   Ⓓ $x = 10, y = 10$

7. Solve the system:

   $x = 13 + 2y$
   $x - 2y = 13$

   Ⓐ $x = 0, y = 13$
   Ⓑ $x = 13, y = 0$
   Ⓒ There is no solution.
   Ⓓ There are infinitely many solutions.

8. Solve the system:

   $y = 3x - 7$
   $x + y = 9$

   Ⓐ $x = 3, y = 6$
   Ⓑ $x = 4, y = 5$
   Ⓒ $x = 5, y = 4$
   Ⓓ $x = 6, y = 3$

9. Solve the system:

   $2x + 5y = 12$
   $2x + 5y = 9$

   Ⓐ $x = 1, y = 2$
   Ⓑ $x = 2, y = 1$
   Ⓒ There is no solution.
   Ⓓ There are infinitely many solutions.

10. Solve the system:

    -4x + 7y = 26
    4x + 7y = 2

    Ⓐ x = -3, y = 2
    Ⓑ x = 3, y = -2
    Ⓒ x = -2, y = 3
    Ⓓ x = 2, y = -3

11. Randy has to raise $50.00 to repair his bicycle. He is only $1.00 short. He has only $1 and $5 bills. If he has one more $1 bills than $5 bills, how many does he have of each?

    Ⓐ Ten $1-bills, Nine $5-bills
    Ⓑ Nine $1-bills and Eight $5-bills
    Ⓒ Eight $1-bills and Seven $5-bills
    Ⓓ Seven $1-bills and Six $5-bills

12. Anya is three years older than her brother, Cole. In 11 years, Cole will be twice Anya's current age. Find their current ages.

    Ⓐ Anya: 11 years old, Cole: 8 years old
    Ⓑ Anya: 10 years old, Cole: 7 years old
    Ⓒ Anya: 9 years old, Cole: 6 years old
    Ⓓ Anya: 8 years old, Cole: 5 years old

CHAPTER 2 → Lesson 13: Systems of Equations in Real-World Problems

1. Jorge and Jillian have cell phones with different service providers. Jorge pays $50 a month and $1 per text message sent. Jillian pays $72 a month and $0.12 per text message sent. How many texts would each of them have to send for their bill to be the same amount at the end of the month?

   Ⓐ 2 texts
   Ⓑ 22 texts
   Ⓒ 25 texts
   Ⓓ 47 texts

2. Mr. Stevens is 63 years older than his grandson, Tom. In 3 years, Mr. Stevens will be four times as old as Tom. How old is Tom?

   Ⓐ 17 years
   Ⓑ 18 years
   Ⓒ 20 years
   Ⓓ 22 years

3. Janet has packed a total of 50 textbooks and workbooks in a box, but she can't remember how many of each are in the box. Each textbook weighs 2 pounds, and each workbook weighs 0.5 pounds, and the total weight of the books in the box is 55 pounds. If t is the number of textbooks and w is the number of workbooks, which of the following systems of equations represents this situation?

   Ⓐ $t + w = 55$
   $2t + 0.5w = 50$

   Ⓑ $2t + w = 50$
   $t + 0.5w = 55$

   Ⓒ $t + w = 50$
   $2t + 0.5w = 55$

   Ⓓ $t + w = 55$
   $2.5(t + w) = 50$

4. Plumber A charges $50 to come to your house, plus $40 per hour of labor. Plumber B charges $75 to come to your house, plus $35 per hour of labor. If y is the total dollar amount charged for x hours of labor, which of the following systems of equations correctly represents this situation?

Ⓐ y = 50x + 40
   y = 75x + 35

Ⓑ y = 50x + 40
   y = 35x + 75

Ⓒ y = 40x + 50
   y = 75x + 35

Ⓓ y = 40x + 50
   y = 35x + 75

5. 10 tacos and 6 drinks cost $19.50. 7 tacos and 5 drinks cost $14.25. If t is the cost of one taco and d is the cost of one drink, which of the following systems of equations represents this situation?

Ⓐ 10t + 6d = 19.50
   7t + 5d = 14.25

Ⓑ 6t + 10d = 19.50
   5t + 7d = 14.25

Ⓒ 10t + 7t = 19.50
   6d + 5d = 14.25

Ⓓ 16(t + d) = 19.50
   12(t + d) = 14.25

6. Cindy has $25 saved and earns $12 per week for walking dogs. Mindy has $55 saved and earns $7 per week for watering plants. Cindy and Mindy save all of the money they earn and do not spend any of their savings. After how many weeks will they have the same amount saved? How much money will they have saved?

Ⓐ After 4 weeks, they each will have $83 saved.
Ⓑ After 5 weeks, they each will have $85 saved.
Ⓒ After 6 weeks, they each will have $97 saved.
Ⓓ After 7 weeks, they each will have $104 saved.

7. The seventh and eighth grade classes are raising money for a field trip. The seventh graders are selling calendars for $1.50 each and the eighth graders are selling candy bars for $1.25 each. If they have sold a combined total of 1100 items and each class has the same income, find the number of each item that has been sold.

   Ⓐ 400 calendars and 700 candy bars
   Ⓑ 700 calendars and 400 candy bars
   Ⓒ 500 calendars and 600 candy bars
   Ⓓ 600 calendars and 500 candy bars

8. Anya is three years older than her brother, Cole. In 11 years, Cole will be twice Anya's current age. Find their current ages.

   Ⓐ Anya: 11 years old
      Cole: 8 years old
   Ⓑ Anya: 10 years old
      Cole: 7 years old
   Ⓒ Anya: 9 years old
      Cole: 6 years old
   Ⓓ Anya: 8 years old
      Cole: 5 years old

9. Tom and his sister both decided to get part-time jobs after school at competing clothing stores. Tom makes $15 an hour and receives $3 in commission for every item he sells. His sister makes $7 an hour and receives $5 in commission for every item she sells. How many items would each of them have to sell to make the same amount of money in an hour?

   Ⓐ 1 item
   Ⓑ 2 items
   Ⓒ 3 items
   Ⓓ 4 items

10. Lucia and Jack are training for a marathon. Lucia started the first day by running 2 miles and adds 0.25 mile to her distance every day. Jack started the first day by running 0.5 mile and adds 0.5 mile to his distance every day. If both continue this plan, on what day will Lucia and Jack run the same distance?

    Ⓐ Day 3
    Ⓑ Day 7
    Ⓒ Day 9
    Ⓓ Day 12

11. The admission fee at a carnival is $3.00 for children and $5.00 for adults. On the first day 1,500 people enter the fair and $5740 is collected. How many children and how many adults attended the carnival?

Select the correct system and answer. There can be more than one correct answer, choose all applicable ones.

Ⓐ $\begin{cases} 3c + 5a = 1500 \\ c + a = 5740 \end{cases}$

Ⓑ $\begin{cases} 3c + 5a = 5740 \\ c + a = 1500 \end{cases}$

Ⓒ $a = 620, c = 880$
Ⓓ $a = 936, c = 564$

12. Match the correct solution to the corresponding word problem.

	15 and 19	$1.50 and $1.05	$1.75 and $1.60	18 and 31
1. You buy 5 bags of chips and 9 bags of pretzels for $16.95. Later you buy 10 bags of chips and 10 bags of pretzels for $25.50. Find the cost of 1 bag of chips and 1 bag of pretzels.				
2. You empty your coin jar and find 49 coins (all nickels and quarter). The total value of the coins is $8.65. Find the number of nickels and quarters.				
3. Jill bought one hot dog and two soft drinks for a cost of $4.95. Jack bought three hot dogs and one soft drink for a cost of $6.85. Find the cost of one hot dog and one soft drink.				
4. There are a total of 34 lions and hyenas. Each lion eats 4 antelope. Each hyena eats 3 antelope. 117 antelope are eaten. Find the number of lions and hyenas.				

End of Algebraic Reasoning

Chapter 3
Geometric Reasoning

Lesson 1: Pythagorean Theorem in Real-World Problems

1. The bottom of a 17-foot ladder is placed on level ground 8 feet from the side of a house as shown in the figure below. Find the vertical height at which the top of the ladder touches the side of the house.

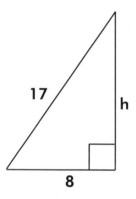

- Ⓐ h = 9 feet
- Ⓑ h = 12 feet
- Ⓒ h = 15 feet
- Ⓓ h = 18 feet

2. Which of the following equations could be used to find the value of w?

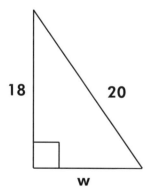

- Ⓐ $w^2 + 18^2 = 20^2$
- Ⓑ $18^2 - w^2 = 20^2$
- Ⓒ $20^2 + 18^2 = w^2$
- Ⓓ $w + 18 = 20$

3. John has a chest where he keeps his antiques. What is the measure of the diagonal (d) of John's chest with the height (c) = 3ft, width (b) = 3ft, and length (a) = 5ft.?

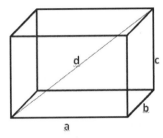

Ⓐ $\sqrt{42}$ ft²
Ⓑ $\sqrt{44}$ ft²
Ⓒ $\sqrt{34}$ ft
Ⓓ $\sqrt{43}$ ft

4. Mary has a lawn that has a width (a) of 30 yards, and a length (b) of 40 yards. What is the measurement of the diagonal (c) of the lawn?

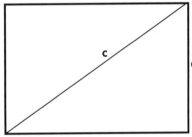

Ⓐ 50 yards
Ⓑ 49 yards
Ⓒ 51 yards
Ⓓ 50 yards²

5. A construction company needed to build a sign with the width (a) of 9 ft, and a length (b) of 20 ft. What will be the approximate measurement of the diagonal (c) of the sign?

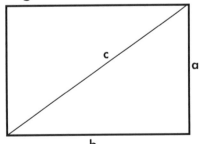

Ⓐ 23 ft
Ⓑ 22 ft
Ⓒ 20 ft
Ⓓ 19 ft

6. An unofficial baseball diamond is measured to be 50 yards wide. What is the approximate measurement of one side (a) of the diamond?

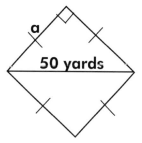

  Ⓐ 34 ft
  Ⓑ 35 yards
  Ⓒ 35 ft
  Ⓓ 36 yards

7. The neighborhood swimming pool is 20 ft wide and 30 ft long. What is the approximate measurement of the diagonal (d) of the base of the pool?

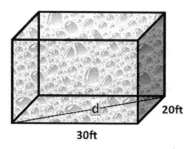

  Ⓐ 36 ft
  Ⓑ 35 ft
  Ⓒ 34 ft
  Ⓓ 34 yards

8. To get to her friend's house, a student must walk 20 feet to the corner of their streets, turn left and walk 15 feet to her friend's house.
How much shorter would it be if she could cut across a neighbor's yard and walk a straight line from her house to her friend's house?

  Ⓐ 5 feet shorter
  Ⓑ 10 feet shorter
  Ⓒ 25 feet shorter
  Ⓓ 35 feet shorter

9. Your school principal wants the custodian to put a new flag up on the flagpole. If the flagpole is 40 feet tall and they have a 50 foot ladder, approximately how far from the base of the pole can he place the base of his ladder in order to accomplish the task?

Ⓐ Up to 10 ft away
Ⓑ Up to 20 ft away
Ⓒ Up to 30 ft away
Ⓓ Up to 40 ft away

10. Your kite is at the end of a 50 ft string. You are 25 ft from the outside wall of a building that you know makes a right angle with the ground.
How high is the kite approximately?

Ⓐ Approximately 39 ft high
Ⓑ Approximately 40 ft high
Ⓒ Approximately 42 ft high
Ⓓ Approximately 43 ft high

11. Match the following word problem with the correct equation that you would use to solve it.

	$9^2+x^2=15^2$	$40^2+38^2=x^2$	$9^2+15^2=x^2$	$x^2+38^2=40^2$
One house is 15 miles due north of the park. Another house is 9 miles due east of the park. How far apart are the houses from each other?	○	○	○	○
The foot of a ladder is put 9 feet from the wall. If the ladder is 15 feet long how high up the building will the ladder reach?	○	○	○	○
If you drive your car 40 miles south and then 38 miles east, how far would the shortest route be from your starting point?	○	○	○	○
The diagonal of a TV is 40 inches. The TV is 38 inches long. How tall is the TV?	○	○	○	○

12. Fill in the missing information needed to solve for the word problem. Round to the nearest tenth if necessary.

WORD PROBLEM	LEG(a)	LEG(b)	HYPOTENUSE(c)
Find the height of a pyramid whose slant height is 26 cm and base length is 48 cm	24		
Find the base length of a pyramid whose height is 8 in and slant height 17 in.		8	17
The foot of a ladder is put 5 feet from the wall. If the top of the ladder is 10 feet from the ground, how long is the ladder?		10	

13. On a bike ride you start at your house and ride your bike 3.5 miles north and then 1.25 miles east. How far are you directly from your house? Select the correct equation with the correct solution to match the word problem.

Ⓐ $\sqrt{3.5^2 + 1.25^2} = 22.56$ mi
Ⓑ $\sqrt{3.5^2 - 1.25^2} = 3.34$ mi
Ⓒ $\sqrt{3.5^2 + 1.25^2} = 3.72$ mi

CHAPTER 3 → Lesson 2: Pythagorean Theorem & Coordinate System

1. A robot begins at point A, travels 4 meters west, then turns and travels 7 meters south, reaching point B. What is the approximate straight-line distance between points A and B?

   Ⓐ 8 meters
   Ⓑ 9 meters
   Ⓒ 10 meters
   Ⓓ 11 meters

2. What is the distance between the points (1, 3) and (9, 9)?

   Ⓐ 6 units
   Ⓑ 8 units
   Ⓒ 10 units
   Ⓓ 12 units

3. Find the distance (approximately) between Pt A (2, 7) and Pt B (-2, -7).

   Ⓐ 14.0
   Ⓑ 14.6
   Ⓒ 18.0
   Ⓓ 13.4

4. Find the distance (approximately) between Pt P (5, 3) and the origin (0, 0).

   Ⓐ 4.0
   Ⓑ 5.1
   Ⓒ 5.8
   Ⓓ 8.0

5. Find the distance (approximately) between the points A (11, 12) and B (7, 8).

   Ⓐ 4.0
   Ⓑ 5.3
   Ⓒ 5.7
   Ⓓ 8.0

6. Is it closer to go from Pt A (4, 6) to Pt B (2, -4) or Pt A to Pt C (-5, 2)?

   Ⓐ A to B
   Ⓑ A to C
   Ⓒ Neither, they are both the same distance.
   Ⓓ Not enough information.

7. Paul lives 50 yards east and 40 yards south of his friend, Larry. If he wants to shorten his walk by walking in a straight line from his home to Larry's, how far (approximately) will he walk?

   Ⓐ 64 yards
   Ⓑ 62 yards
   Ⓒ 60 yards
   Ⓓ 58 yards

8. In a coordinate plane, a point P (7,8) is rotated 90° clockwise around the origin and then reflected across the vertical axis. Find the distance (approximately) between the original point and the final point.

   Ⓐ 14 units
   Ⓑ 21 units
   Ⓒ 24 units
   Ⓓ None of the above

9. You are using a coordinate plane to sketch out a plan for your vegetable garden. Your garden will be a rectangle 15 ft wide and 20 ft long. You want a square in the center with 3 ft sides to be reserved for flowers. If the garden is plotted on the coordinate plane with the southwest corner at the origin, what are the coordinates of the center of the flower garden? (Assume that the longer side is placed on the y-axis)

   Ⓐ (15, 10)
   Ⓑ (7.5, 10)
   Ⓒ (-15, 10)
   Ⓓ (-7.5, 10)

10. You are using a coordinate plane to sketch out a plan for a vegetable garden. The garden will be a rectangle 15 feet wide and 20 feet long. You want a square in the center with 3 feet sides to be reserved for flowers. The garden is plotted in the coordinate grid so that the southwest corner is placed at the origin. Find the length of the diagonal (approximately) of the flower bed.

   Ⓐ 4.0 feet
   Ⓑ 4.2 feet
   Ⓒ 5.0 feet
   Ⓓ 5.2 feet

11. Match the ordered pairs with the approximate distance between them.

	10.8	12.2	13	14.8
(6, 5) and (-4, 9)	○	○	○	○
(-8, 0) and (5, -7)	○	○	○	○
(-4, -9) and (6, -2)	○	○	○	○
(5, 4) and (12, 15)	○	○	○	○

12. Given below are the coordinates of the hypotenuse of right-angled triangles. Fill in the missing values with the lengths of the sides. Round to the nearest hundredth if necessary.

ORDERED PAIRS	LEG LENGTH	LEG LENGTH	HYPOTENUSE
(6,2),(0,-6)	6		
(-3,-1),(-4,0)	1	1	
(-2,3),(-1,7)			4.12

CHAPTER 3 → Lesson 3: Verifying the Pythagorean Theorem

1. Which of the following could be the lengths of the sides of a right triangle?

   Ⓐ 1, 2, 3
   Ⓑ 2, 3, 4
   Ⓒ 3, 4, 5
   Ⓓ 4, 5, 6

2. A triangle has sides 8 cm long and 15 cm long, with a 90° angle between them. What is the length of the third side?

   Ⓐ 7 cm
   Ⓑ 17 cm
   Ⓒ 23 cm
   Ⓓ 289 cm

3. Find the value of c, rounded to the nearest tenth.

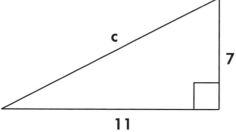

   Ⓐ 8.5
   Ⓑ 8.8
   Ⓒ 13.0
   Ⓓ 19.3

4. A square has sides 5 inches long. What is the approximate length of a diagonal of the square?

   Ⓐ 5 inches
   Ⓑ 6 inches
   Ⓒ 7 inches
   Ⓓ 8 inches

5. Which of the following INCORRECTLY completes this statement of the Pythagorean theorem?
   In a right triangle with legs of lengths a and b and hypotenuse of length c, ...

   Ⓐ $a^2 + b^2 = c^2$
   Ⓑ $c^2 - a^2 = b^2$
   Ⓒ $c^2 - b^2 = a^2$
   Ⓓ $a^2 + c^2 = b^2$

6. A Pythagorean triplet is a set of three positive integers a, b, and c that satisfy the equation $a^2 + b^2 = c^2$. Which of the following is a Pythagorean triple?

   Ⓐ a = 3, b = 6, c = 9
   Ⓑ a = 6, b = 9, c = 12
   Ⓒ a = 9, b = 12, c = 15
   Ⓓ a = 12, b = 15, c = 18

7. If an isosceles right triangle has legs of 4 inches each, find the length of the hypotenuse.

   Ⓐ Approximately 6 in.
   Ⓑ Approximately 5 in.
   Ⓒ Approximately 4 in.
   Ⓓ Approximately 3 in.

8. In triangle ABC, angle C = 90°, AC = 4 and AB = 10. Find BC to the nearest tenth.

   Ⓐ 9.5
   Ⓑ 9.2
   Ⓒ 8.9
   Ⓓ 8.5

9. In triangle ABC, angle C = 90°, AB = 35, and BC = 28. Find AC.

   Ⓐ 23
   Ⓑ 22
   Ⓒ 21
   Ⓓ 20

10. The diagonal of a square is 25. Find the approximate side lengths.

   Ⓐ 15
   Ⓑ 16
   Ⓒ 17
   Ⓓ 18

11. You have a right triangle with leg lengths of 6 and 8. What is the length of the hypotenuse? Fill in the numbers into the equation and solve.

$6^2 + 8^2 = C^2$
$100 = C^2$
$\sqrt{100} = C$
$C = ?$

12. Which equation would you use to solve for the missing side of the triangle pictured below?

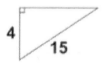

4

15

Ⓐ $4^2 + 15^2 = x^2$
Ⓑ $4^2 + x^2 = 15^2$
Ⓒ $x^2 + 15^2 = 4^2$

CHAPTER 3 → Lesson 4: Angles

1. **Find x.**

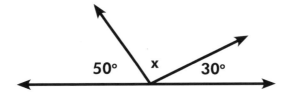

- Ⓐ 40°
- Ⓑ 60°
- Ⓒ 80°
- Ⓓ 100°

2. **Find the measures of the missing angles in the figure below.**

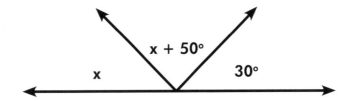

- Ⓐ 30° and 60°
- Ⓑ 60° and 90°
- Ⓒ 50° and 100°
- Ⓓ 60° and 120°

3. **The sum of the measures of angles a and b 155 degrees. What is the measure of angle b?**

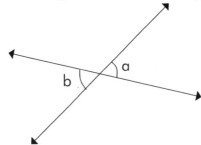

- Ⓐ 155 degrees
- Ⓑ 77.5 degrees
- Ⓒ 35 degrees
- Ⓓ 210.5 degrees

4. What is true about every pair of vertical angles?

Ⓐ They are supplementary.
Ⓑ They are complementary.
Ⓒ They are equal in measure.
Ⓓ They total 360 degrees.

5. If the sum of the measures of two angles is 180 degrees, they are called —

Ⓐ supplementary angles
Ⓑ complementary angles
Ⓒ vertical angles
Ⓓ equivalent angles

6. If angle a measures 30 degrees, what is the measure of angle b?

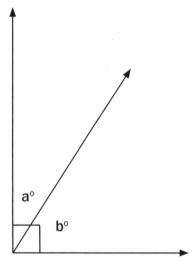

Ⓐ 60 degrees
Ⓑ 30 degrees
Ⓒ 150 degrees
Ⓓ 20 degrees

7. If the measure of the first of two complementary angles is 68 degrees, what is the measure of the second angle?

Ⓐ 68 degrees
Ⓑ 22 degrees
Ⓒ 44 degrees
Ⓓ 34 degrees

8. If the sum of the measures of angles a and b is 110 degrees, what is the measure of angle c?

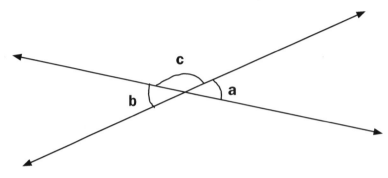

   - Ⓐ 125 degrees
   - Ⓑ 55 degrees
   - Ⓒ 70 degrees
   - Ⓓ 180 degrees

9. If two angles are both supplementary and equal in measure, they must be

   - Ⓐ vertical angles
   - Ⓑ right angles
   - Ⓒ adjacent angles
   - Ⓓ obtuse angles

10. If the sum of the measures of angles a and b is 240 degrees, what is the measure of angle c?

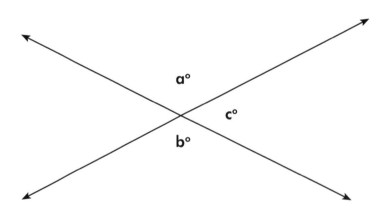

   - Ⓐ 60 degrees
   - Ⓑ 30 degrees
   - Ⓒ 160 degrees
   - Ⓓ 150 degrees

11. What is the measure of angle ∠ A? Type the answer in the box.

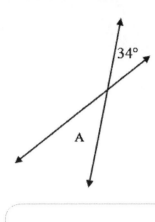

12. What is the measure of angle ∠ A? Type the answer in the box.

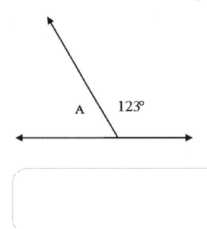

13. What is the measure of angle ∠ A? Type the answer in the box.

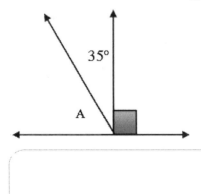

CHAPTER 3 → Lesson 5: Interior & Exterior Angles in Geometric Figures

1. What term describes a pair of angles formed by the intersection of two straight lines that share a common vertex but do not share any common sides?

    Ⓐ Supplementary Angles
    Ⓑ Complementary Angles
    Ⓒ Horizontal Angles
    Ⓓ Vertical Angles

2. If a triangle has two angles with measures that add up to 100 degrees, what must the measure of the third angle be?

    Ⓐ 180 degrees
    Ⓑ 100 degrees
    Ⓒ 80 degrees
    Ⓓ 45 degrees

3.

    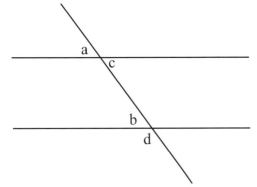

    The figure shows two parallel lines intersected by a third line. If a = 55°, what is the value of b?

    Ⓐ 35°
    Ⓑ 45°
    Ⓒ 55°
    Ⓓ 125°

4.

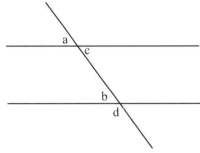

The figure shows two parallel lines intersected by a third line. If b = 60°, what is the value of c?

Ⓐ 30°
Ⓑ 60°
Ⓒ 90°
Ⓓ 120°

5.

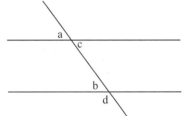

The figure shows two parallel lines intersected by a third line. If d = 130°, what is the value of a?

Ⓐ 30°
Ⓑ 40°
Ⓒ 50°
Ⓓ 130°

6.

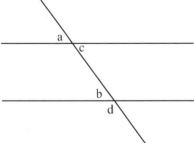

The figure shows two parallel lines intersected by a third line. Which of the following angles are equal in measure?

Ⓐ a and b only
Ⓑ a and c only
Ⓒ b and c only
Ⓓ a, b, and c

7. Two angles in a triangle measure 65° each. What is the measure of the third angle in the triangle?

Ⓐ 25°
Ⓑ 50°
Ⓒ 65°
Ⓓ 130°

8.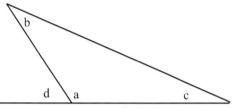

If b = 40° and c = 30°, what is the measure of d?

Ⓐ 35°
Ⓑ 70°
Ⓒ 110°
Ⓓ 145°

9. In right triangle ABC, Angle C is the right angle. Angle A measures 70°. Find the measure of the exterior angle at angle C.

Ⓐ 180°
Ⓑ 90°
Ⓒ 110°
Ⓓ 160°

10. If two parallel lines are cut by a transversal, the alternate interior angles are _____.

Ⓐ supplementary
Ⓑ complementary
Ⓒ equal in measure
Ⓓ none of the above

11. **Match the figure with the sum of the interior angles of each polygon.**

	2520	1080	1440	4140	540
Decagon	○	○	○	○	○
16-gon	○	○	○	○	○
Pentagon	○	○	○	○	○
25-gon	○	○	○	○	○
Octagon	○	○	○	○	○

12. **Observe the figure given below. ∠3 and ∠7 are what type of angles?**

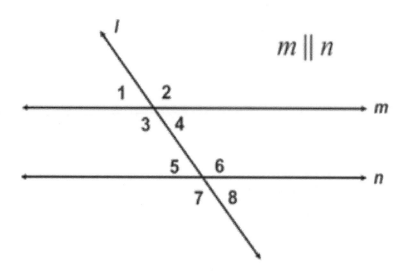

$m \parallel n$

∠3 and ∠7 are what type of angles? Write your answer in the box given below.

CHAPTER 3 → Lesson 6: Interior Angles of Regular Polygons

1. **What is the number and sum of the interior angles of a triangle?**

   Ⓐ 3 & 90 degrees
   Ⓑ 3 & 180 degrees
   Ⓒ 4 & 270 degrees
   Ⓓ 6 & 360 degrees

2. **What is the formula to calculate the sum of the interior angles of a regular polygon with n sides?**

   Ⓐ Sum=(n−2)×180°
   Ⓑ Sum=(n+2)×180°
   Ⓒ Sum=n×180°
   Ⓓ Sum=(n−1)×180°

3. **What is the sum of the interior angles of a hexagon?**

   Ⓐ 180 degrees
   Ⓑ 360 degrees
   Ⓒ 540 degrees
   Ⓓ 720 degrees

4. **What is the sum of the interior angles of a pentagon?**

   Ⓐ 360 degrees
   Ⓑ 450 degrees
   Ⓒ 540 degrees
   Ⓓ 720 degrees

5. **If the measure of each interior angle of a regular hexagon is 120 degrees, how many sides does the hexagon have?**

   Ⓐ 4 sides
   Ⓑ 5 sides
   Ⓒ 6 sides
   Ⓓ 7 sides

6. A regular octagon has an interior angle of 135 degrees. What is the sum of its interior angles?

   Ⓐ 1080°
   Ⓑ 1440°
   Ⓒ 720°
   Ⓓ 900°

7. The interior angle of a regular polygon measures 150 degrees. How many sides does the polygon have?

   Ⓐ 8 sides
   Ⓑ 9 sides
   Ⓒ 10 sides
   Ⓓ 12 sides

8. The sum of the interior angles of a regular polygon is 1440 degrees. How many sides does the polygon have?

   Ⓐ 6 sides
   Ⓑ 8 sides
   Ⓒ 9 sides
   Ⓓ 10 sides

9. What is the measure of each interior angle of a regular heptagon?

   Ⓐ 128.57°
   Ⓑ 120°
   Ⓒ 135.23°
   Ⓓ 150°

10. The interior angle of a regular polygon is 160 degrees. What is the measure of each exterior angle?

   Ⓐ 20°
   Ⓑ 30°
   Ⓒ 40°
   Ⓓ 50°

CHAPTER 3 → Lesson 7: Transformations of Points and Lines

1. The point (4, 3) is rotated 90° clockwise about the origin. What are the coordinates of the resulting point?

   Ⓐ (-3, 4)
   Ⓑ (-4, 3)
   Ⓒ (4, -3)
   Ⓓ (3, -4)

2. A line segment has a length of 9 units. After a certain transformation is applied to the segment, the new segment has a length of 9 units. What was the transformation?

   Ⓐ A rotation
   Ⓑ A reflection
   Ⓒ A translation
   Ⓓ Any of the above transformations.

3. The point (2, 4) is rotated 180° clockwise about the origin. What are the coordinates of the resulting point?

   Ⓐ (-2, -4)
   Ⓑ (-2, 4)
   Ⓒ (2, -4)
   Ⓓ (2, 4)

4. Two points are located in the (x, y) plane on the opposite sides of the y-axis. After a certain transformation is applied to both points, the two new points end up again on the opposite sides of the y-axis. What was the transformation?

   Ⓐ A rotation
   Ⓑ A reflection
   Ⓒ A translation
   Ⓓ A dilation

5. A certain transformation is applied to a line segment. The new segment shifted to the left within the coordinate plane. What was the transformation?

   Ⓐ A rotation
   Ⓑ A reflection
   Ⓒ A translation
   Ⓓ It cannot be determined.

6. A line segment with end points (1, 1) and (5, 5) is moved and the new end points are now (1, 5) and (5,1). Which transformation took place?

Ⓐ reflection
Ⓑ rotation
Ⓒ translation
Ⓓ dilation

7. A certain transformation moves a line segment as follows: A (2, 1) moves to A' (2, -1) and B (5, 3) to B' (5, -3).
Name this transformation.

Ⓐ Rotation
Ⓑ Translation
Ⓒ Reflection
Ⓓ Dilation

8. After a certain transformation is applied to point (x, y), it moves to (y, -x).
Name the transformation.

Ⓐ Rotation
Ⓑ Translation
Ⓒ Reflection
Ⓓ Dilation

9. A transformation moves the point (0, y) to a new location at (0, -y).
Name this transformation.

Ⓐ Rotation
Ⓑ Translation
Ⓒ Reflection
Ⓓ It could be any one of the three listed.

10. (x,y) is in Quadrant 1. Reflection across the y-axis would move it to a point with the following coordinates.

Ⓐ (x, y)
Ⓑ (-x, -y)
Ⓒ (x, -y)
Ⓓ (-x, y)

11. Mark **TRUE** or **FALSE** based on the description of the transformation.

	TRUE	FALSE
If you graph a point A (3,2). The point gets translated 10 units down, it will end up at A'(3,12)	○	○
Point A (-2,4) is reflected over the y-axis. The new ordered pair will be A'(2,4).	○	○
Line AB is 3 units long. After it is rotated 90° counter clockwise, the line segment will now be 3 units long.	○	○
Point A(5,8) is translated 3 units to the right. It is now located at A'(8,8)	○	○

12. Enter the correct operation that will describe the rule for the translation left 3 units and up 4 units?

(x,y) --> (x ☐ 3, y ☐ 4)

13. Circle the graph that represents a rotation.

Ⓐ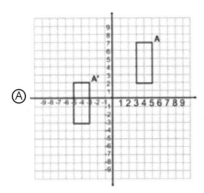

Ⓑ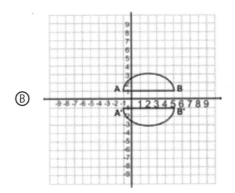

Ⓒ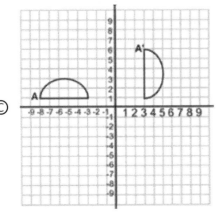

CHAPTER 3 → Lesson 8: Transformations of Angles

1. △**ABC** is reflected across the x-axis.
    Which two angles are congruent?

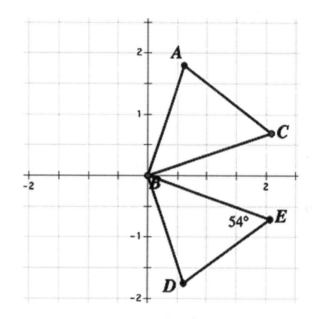

    Ⓐ ∠ A and ∠ C
    Ⓑ ∠ A and ∠ E
    Ⓒ ∠ C and ∠ D
    Ⓓ ∠ C and ∠ E

2. △**ABC** is rotated 90°.
    Which two angles are congruent?

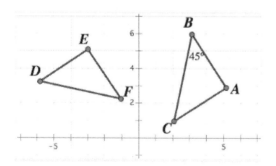

    Ⓐ ∠ A and ∠ C
    Ⓑ ∠ B and ∠ E
    Ⓒ ∠ C and ∠ D
    Ⓓ ∠ C and ∠ F

3. What rigid transformation should be used to prove $\angle ABC \cong \angle XYZ$?

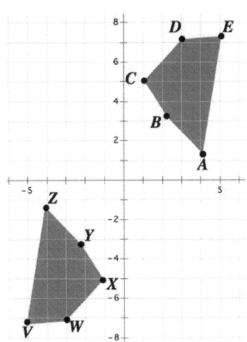

Ⓐ Reflection
Ⓑ Rotation
Ⓒ Translation
Ⓓ None of the above

4. What rigid transformation should be used to prove $\angle ABC \cong \angle XYZ$?

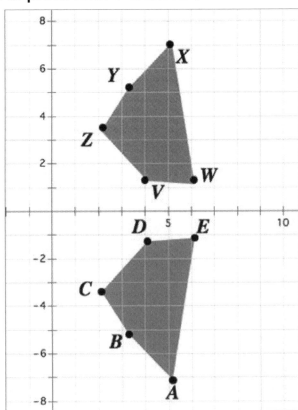

Ⓐ Reflection
Ⓑ Rotation
Ⓒ Translation
Ⓓ None of the above

5. △**ABC** is rotated 90°.
   Which two angles are equivalent?

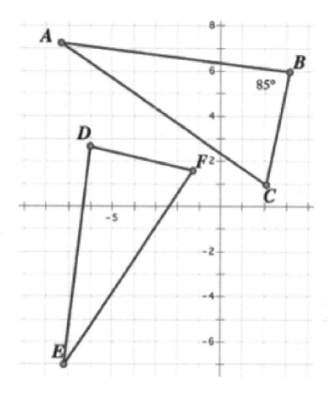

Ⓐ ∠ A and ∠ F
Ⓑ ∠ B and ∠ D
Ⓒ ∠ B and ∠ F
Ⓓ ∠ C and ∠ D

6. If all the triangles below are the result of one or more rigid transformations, which of the following MUST be true?

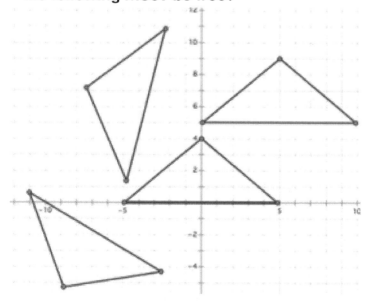

Ⓐ All corresponding line segments are congruent.
Ⓑ All corresponding angles are congruent.
Ⓒ All triangles have the same area.
Ⓓ A,B, and C are all correct.

7. What rigid transformation should be used to prove $\angle ABC \cong \angle DEF$?

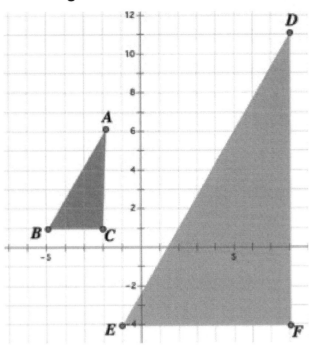

Ⓐ Reflection
Ⓑ Rotation
Ⓒ Translation
Ⓓ None of the above

8. A company is looking to design a new logo, which consists only of transformations of the angle below:

Which logo meets the company's demand?

Ⓐ

Ⓑ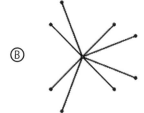

Ⓒ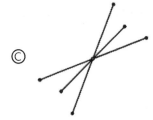

Ⓓ All of the above

9. The angle ∠ AOB is 45° and has been rotated 120° around point C. What is the measure of the new angle ∠ XYZ?

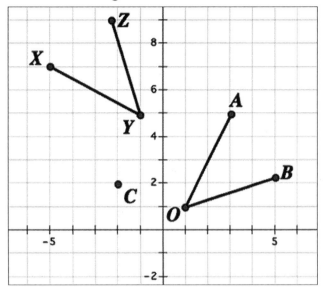

Ⓐ 30°
Ⓑ 45°
Ⓒ 90°
Ⓓ 120°

10. Find the measure of ∠ ABC

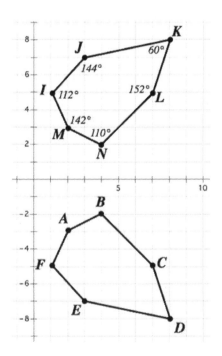

Ⓐ 110°
Ⓑ 112°
Ⓒ 142°
Ⓓ 144°

11. Select the angle measure that corresponds with each transformation. Your preimage has an angle measure of 30°

	30°	60°	90°
Translation	○	○	○
Reflection	○	○	○
Rotation	○	○	○
Dilation	○	○	○

12. In the figure below $\triangle ABC \cong \triangle DEF$. . Which angle will correspond with angle B? Type the letter (in capitals) which corresponds to the required angle in the box.

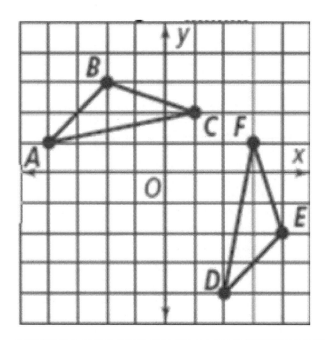

13. Triangle ABC is rotated 90° counterclockwise. Which two angles would be congruent?

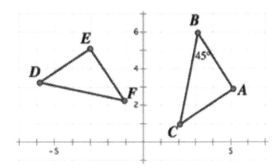

Ⓐ Angle A and Angle C
Ⓑ Angle B and Angle E
Ⓒ Angle C and Angle D
Ⓓ Angle C and Angle F

CHAPTER 3 → Lesson 9: Transformations of Parallel Lines

1. Two parallel line segments move from Quadrant One to Quadrant Four. Their slopes do not change. What transformation has taken place?

    Ⓐ Reflection
    Ⓑ Translation
    Ⓒ Dilation
    Ⓓ This is not a transformation.

2. Two parallel line segments move from Quadrant One to Quadrant Four. Their slopes change from a positive slope to a negative slope. What transformation has taken place?

    Ⓐ Reflection
    Ⓑ Rotation
    Ⓒ Translation
    Ⓓ It could be either a rotation or a reflection.

3. Two parallel line segments move from Quadrant One to Quadrant Two. Their slopes change from a negative slope to a positive slope. What transformation has taken place?

    Ⓐ Reflection
    Ⓑ Rotation
    Ⓒ Translation
    Ⓓ It could be either a rotation or a reflection.

4. Line L is translated along segment $\overline{AB}$ to create line L'. Will L and L' ever intersect?

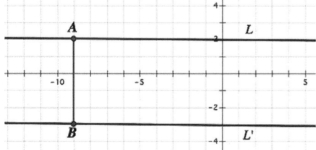

    Ⓐ Yes, line L' is now the same as L.
    Ⓑ Yes, parallel lines always eventually intersect.
    Ⓒ No, every point on L' will always have a corresponding point the distance of $\overline{AB}$ away from L'.
    Ⓓ No, the translation along $\overline{AB}$ does not change the slope from L to L', and lines with the same slope never intersect.

5. Line *L* is translated along segment $\overline{AB}$ to create line *L'*. Will *L* and *L'* ever intersect?

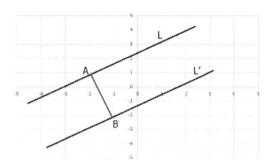

(A) Yes, line *L'* is now the same as *L*.

(B) Yes, parallel lines always eventually intersect.

(C) Yes, every point on *L'* will not always have a corresponding point the distance of AB away from *L'*.

(D) No, the translation along the line segment *AB* does not change the slope from *L* to *L'*, and lines with the same slope never intersect.

6. Line *L* is translated along ray *AC* to create line *L'*. What do you know about the relationship between line *L* and *L'*?

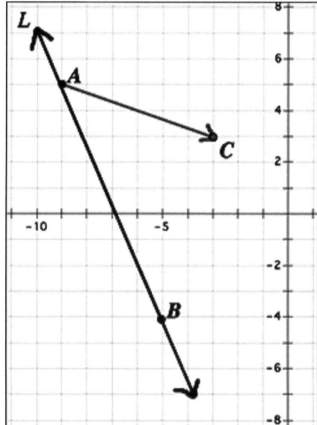

(A) The lines intersect at least once.

(B) The lines are exactly the same.

(C) The lines are parallel.

(D) None of the above.

7. How many lines can be drawn through point *C* that are parallel to line *L*?

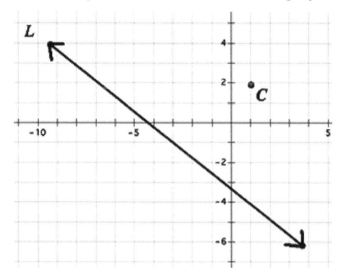

(A) None
(B) One
(C) Two
(D) Infinitely many

8. Figure ABCD is a rectangle that is translated to create WXYZ. Prove $\overline{XY}$ and $\overline{WZ}$ are parallel.

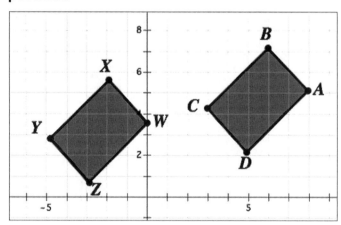

(A) The sides of all rectangles are parallel.

(B) Since *ABCD* is a rectangle, $\overline{AD} \parallel \overline{BC}$. Translations map parallel lines to parallel lines, so $\overline{XY} \parallel \overline{WZ}$.

(C) It cannot be proven because $\overline{XY}$ and $\overline{WZ}$ are perpendicular.

(D) It cannot be proven because the angle of rotation is not given.

9. The two parallel lines shown are rotated 180° abound the origin. What is the result of this transformation?

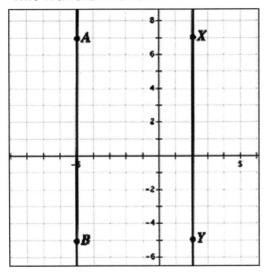

Ⓐ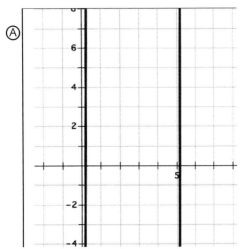

Ⓑ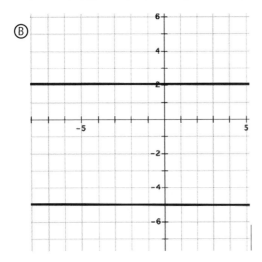

Ⓒ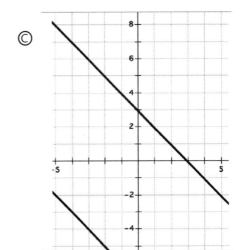

Ⓓ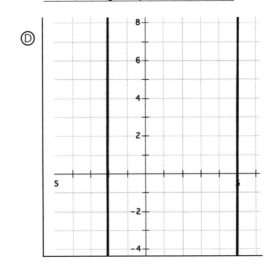

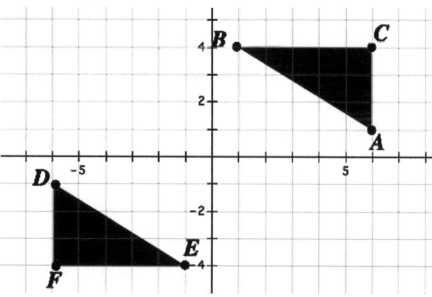

10. Figure *DEF* is the result of 180° rotation around the origin of figure *ABC*. Prove $\overline{AB}$ and $\overline{DE}$ are parallel.

Ⓐ A 180° rotation of a given segment always maps to a parallel segment. Therefore $\overline{AB} \parallel \overline{DE}$.

Ⓑ Corresponding sides of triangles are always parallel. Therefore, $\overline{AB} \parallel \overline{DE}$.

Ⓒ It cannot be proven because $\overline{AB}$ and $\overline{DE}$ are perpendicular.

Ⓓ It cannot be proven due to the angle of rotation is not given.

11. Select what concepts are preserved under these different transformations. Select all that apply.

	Lengths of sides	Angle Measures	Parallel Sides on Figure
Translation	○	○	○
Reflection	○	○	○
Rotation	○	○	○
Dilation	○	○	○

12. Figure ABCD undergoes the shown transformation. The slope of $\overline{AC}$ is $-\frac{1}{3}$. What is the slope of A'C'?

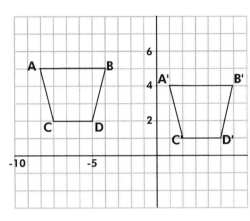

Slope of A'C' is ☐

13. Select the one that correctly shows the parallel lines that have been correctly reflected over the y-axis.

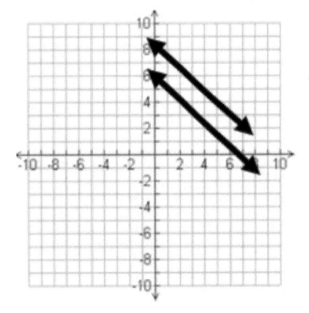

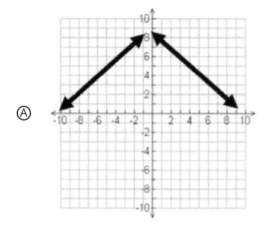

Ⓐ

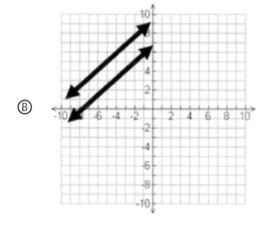

Ⓑ

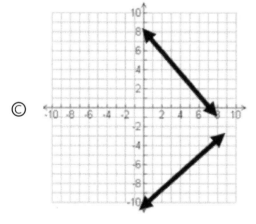

Ⓒ

CHAPTER 3 → Lesson 10: Transformations of Congruency

1. Which of the following examples best represents congruency in nature?

    Ⓐ A mother bear and her cub.
    Ⓑ The wings of a butterfly.
    Ⓒ The tomatoes were picked from my garden.
    Ⓓ The clouds in the sky.

2. If triangle ABC is drawn on a coordinate plane and then reflected over the vertical axis, which of the following statements is true?

    Ⓐ The reflected triangle will be similar ONLY to the original.
    Ⓑ The reflected triangle will be congruent to the original.
    Ⓒ The reflected triangle will be larger than the original.
    Ⓓ The reflected triangle will be smaller than the original.

3. What transformation was applied to the object in quadrant 2 to render the results in the graph below?

    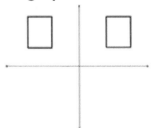

    Ⓐ reflection
    Ⓑ rotation
    Ⓒ translation
    Ⓓ not enough information

4. What transformation was applied to the object in quadrant 2 to render the results in the graph below?

    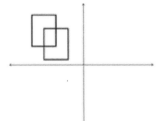

    Ⓐ reflection
    Ⓑ rotation
    Ⓒ translation
    Ⓓ not enough information

5. What is **NOT** true about the graph below?

Ⓐ The object in quadrant 3 could not be a reflection of the object in quadrant 2.
Ⓑ The object in quadrant 3 could be a translation of the object in quadrant 2.
Ⓒ The two objects are congruent.
Ⓓ The object in quadrant 3 could not be a dilation of the object in quadrant 2.

6. Finish the statement. Two congruent objects _____.

Ⓐ have the same dimensions.
Ⓑ have different measured angles.
Ⓒ are not the same shape.
Ⓓ only apply to two-dimensional objects.

7. What transformations can be applied to an object to create a congruent object?

Ⓐ all transformations
Ⓑ dilation and rotation
Ⓒ translation and dilation
Ⓓ reflection, translation, and rotation

8. A figure formed by rotation followed by reflection of an original triangle will be _____.

Ⓐ similar only and not congruent to the original.
Ⓑ congruent to the original.
Ⓒ smaller than the original.
Ⓓ larger than the original.

9. Which of the following is **NOT** a characteristic of congruent triangles?

Ⓐ They have three pairs of congruent sides.
Ⓑ They have three pairs of congruent angles.
Ⓒ Their areas are equal.
Ⓓ They have four pairs of proportional sides

10. Which of the following letters looks the same after a reflection followed by a 180° rotation.

    Ⓐ P
    Ⓑ O
    Ⓒ F
    Ⓓ None of the above.

11. Select all that apply to this transformation.

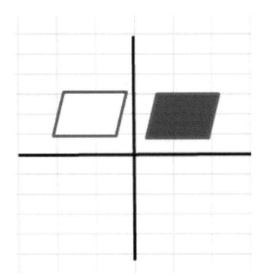

	Apply	Doesn't Apply
the two shapes are congruent	○	○
the two shapes are not congruent	○	○
the two shapes are similar	○	○
the two shapes have the same size	○	○
one shape is rotated from the other shape	○	○
one shape is reflected from the other shape	○	○
one shape is translated from the other shape	○	○

LumosLearning.com

12. Quadrilateral ABCD is translated 5 units to the left and 4 units down. Which congruent quadrilateral match this transformation?

Write your answer in the box given below

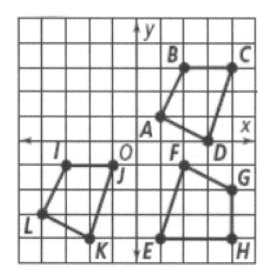

CHAPTER 3 → Lesson 11: Analyzing Transformations

1. **Which of the following transformations could transform triangle A to triangle B?**

    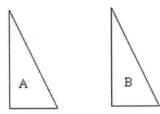

    Ⓐ Rotation
    Ⓑ Reflection
    Ⓒ Translation
    Ⓓ Dilation

2. **Which of the following transformations could transform triangle A to triangle B?**

    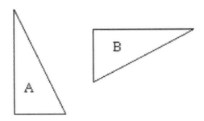

    Ⓐ Rotation
    Ⓑ Reflection
    Ⓒ Translation
    Ⓓ Dilation

3. **Which of the following transformations could transform triangle A to triangle B?**

    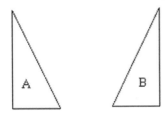

    Ⓐ Rotation
    Ⓑ Reflection
    Ⓒ Translation
    Ⓓ Dilation

4. Which of the following transformations could transform triangle A to triangle B in a single step?

  Ⓐ Rotation
  Ⓑ Reflection
  Ⓒ Translation
  Ⓓ None of the above

5. Which of the following transformations could transform triangle A to triangle B?

  Ⓐ Rotation
  Ⓑ Reflection
  Ⓒ Translation
  Ⓓ Dilation

6. Which of the following transformations could transform triangle A to triangle B?

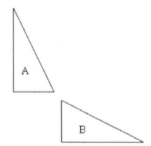

  Ⓐ Rotation
  Ⓑ Reflection
  Ⓒ Translation
  Ⓓ None of the above

7. Which of the following sequences of transformations could transform triangle A to triangle B?

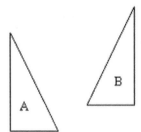

Ⓐ A reflection followed by a translation
Ⓑ A reflection followed by another reflection
Ⓒ A rotation followed by a translation
Ⓓ A dilation followed by a translation

8. Which of the following transformations does NOT preserve congruency?

Ⓐ Rotation
Ⓑ Translation
Ⓒ Reflection
Ⓓ Dilation

9. Consider the triangle with vertices (1, 0), (2, 5) and (-1, 5). Find the vertices of the new triangle after a reflection over the vertical axis followed by a reflection over the horizontal axis.

Ⓐ (-1, 0), (1, 5) and (-2, 5)
Ⓑ (-1, 0), (-2, -5) and (1, -5)
Ⓒ (1, 0), (-2, 5) and (1, 5)
Ⓓ (1, 0), (-2, -5) and (1, -5)

10. Translate the triangle with vertices (1, 0), (2, 5), and (-1, 5), 3 units to the left. Which of the following ordered pairs represent the vertices of the new triangle?

Ⓐ (-2, 0), (-4, 5) and (-1, 5)
Ⓑ (4, 0), (5, 5) and (2, 5)
Ⓒ (-1, 2), (2, 2) and (1, -3)
Ⓓ (-1, 8), (2, 8) and (1, 3)

11. Select the coordinates that will correspond with each transformation for point A.

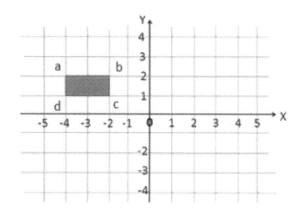

	A(4,-2)	A(-2,1)	A(-4,-2)
Translation (x+2,y-1)	○	○	○
Rotation 180°	○	○	○
Reflection over x-axis	○	○	○

12. In the coordinate plane shown, ΔABC has vertices A(7, 6), B(4, 2), and C(10, 2). What scale factor was used on ΔABC to get ΔDEF.

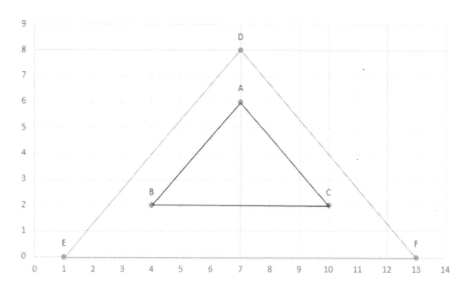

CHAPTER 3 → Lesson 12: Transformations of Similarity

1. Which of the following transformations could transform triangle A to triangle B?

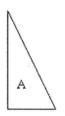

Ⓐ Rotation
Ⓑ Reflection
Ⓒ Translation
Ⓓ Dilation

2. What transformations have been applied to the large object to render the results in the graph below?

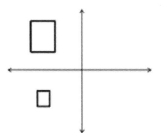

Ⓐ rotation and dilation
Ⓑ rotation and translation
Ⓒ translation and dilation
Ⓓ None of the above

3. What transformations have been applied to the large object to render the results in the graph below?

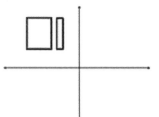

Ⓐ no transformation
Ⓑ reflection and dilation
Ⓒ translation and dilation
Ⓓ rotation and dilation

4. Which graph represents reflection over an axis and dilation?

   Ⓐ

   Ⓑ

   Ⓒ

   Ⓓ None of the above.

5. What transformation is necessary to have two similar, but not congruent, objects?

   Ⓐ Rotation
   Ⓑ Translation
   Ⓒ Dilation
   Ⓓ Reflection

6. Finish this statement. Two similar objects _____.

   Ⓐ have proportional dimensions.
   Ⓑ are always congruent.
   Ⓒ have different measured angles.
   Ⓓ can be different shapes.

7. If a point, P, on a coordinate plane moves from (9, 3) to P' (3, -9) and then to P'' (0, -9), what transformations have been applied?

   Ⓐ Dilation followed by Translation
   Ⓑ Translation followed by Dilation
   Ⓒ Rotation followed by Translation
   Ⓓ Translation followed by Rotation

8. Consider Triangle ABC, where AB = 5, BC = 3, and AC = 6, and Triangle WXY, where WX = 10, XY = 6, and WY = 12.
   Assume ABC is similar to WXY.
   Which of the following represents the ratio of similarity?

   Ⓐ 1 : 2
   Ⓑ 5 : 6
   Ⓒ 3 : 10
   Ⓓ 6 : 20

9. Rectangle A is 1 unit by 2 units.
   Rectangle B is 2 units by 3 units.
   Rectangle C is 2 units by 4 units.
   Rectangle D is 3 units by 6 units.
   Which rectangle is not similar to the other three rectangles?

   Ⓐ A
   Ⓑ B
   Ⓒ C
   Ⓓ D

10. If triangle ABC is similar to triangle WXY and AB = 9, BC = 7, AC = 14, WX = 27, and XY = 21.
    Find WY.

    Ⓐ 44
    Ⓑ 43
    Ⓒ 42
    Ⓓ 41

11. Select which transformations were used to map the pre-image onto the image. Also select if the transformation used leaves the figure congruent or if it only makes them similar.

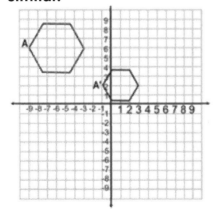

LumosLearning.com

	Used	Similar only	Congruent
Translation	○	○	○
Rotation	○	○	○
Reflection	○	○	○
Dilation	○	○	○

12. The 2 figures are similar. What is the height of the 2nd figure? Write your answer in the box below.

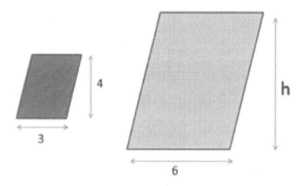

End of Geometric Reasoning

Chapter 4: Data Analysis and Probability

Lesson 1: Interpreting Data Tables & Scatter Plots

1. If a scatter plot has a line of best fit that decreases from left to right, which of the following terms describes the association?

    Ⓐ Positive association
    Ⓑ Negative association
    Ⓒ Constant association
    Ⓓ Nonlinear association

2. If a scatter plot has a line of best fit that increases from left to right, which of the following terms describes the association?

    Ⓐ Positive association
    Ⓑ Negative association
    Ⓒ Constant association
    Ⓓ Nonlinear association

3. Which of the following scatter plots is the best example of a linear association?

    Ⓐ
    Ⓑ
    Ⓒ
    Ⓓ

4. Data for 9 kids' History and English grades are made available in the chart. What is the association between the History and English grades?

Kids	1	2	3	4	5	6	7	8	9
History	63	49	84	33	55	23	71	62	41
English	67	69	82	32	59	26	73	62	39

Ⓐ Positive association
Ⓑ Negative association
Ⓒ Nonlinear association
Ⓓ Constant association

5. Data for 9 kids' History grades and the distance they live from school are made available in the chart. What is the association between these two categories?

Kids	1	2	3	4	5	6	7	8	9
History	63	49	84	33	55	23	71	62	41
Distance from School (miles)	.5	7	3	4	5	2	3	6	9

Ⓐ No association
Ⓑ Positive association
Ⓒ Negative association
Ⓓ Constant association

6. Data for 9 kids' Math and Science grades are made available in the chart. What is the association between the Math and Science grades?

Kids	1	2	3	4	5	6	7	8	9
Science	63	49	84	33	55	23	71	62	41
Math	67	69	82	32	59	26	73	62	39

Ⓐ Positive association
Ⓑ No association
Ⓒ Constant association
Ⓓ Negative association

7. Which of the scatter plots below is the best example of positive association?

Ⓐ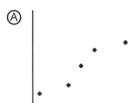

Ⓑ

Ⓒ

Ⓓ

8. **150 students were surveyed and asked whether they played a sport and whether they played a musical instrument. The results are shown in the table below.**

	Plays an Instrument	Does not Plays an Instrument
Plays a Sport	60	30
Does not Plays a Sport	10	50

What percent of the 150 students play a sport and also do not play an instrument?

Ⓐ **20%**
Ⓑ **33%**
Ⓒ **40%**
Ⓓ **50%**

9. 150 students were surveyed and asked whether they played a sport and whether they played a musical instrument. The results are shown in the table below.

	Plays an Instrument	Does not Plays an Instrument
Plays a Sport	60	30
Does not Plays a Sport	10	50

Which of the following statements is NOT supported by the data?

Ⓐ A randomly chosen student who plays a sport is 2 times as likely to play an instrument as to not play an instrument.
Ⓑ A randomly chosen student who does not play an instrument is 2 times as likely to not play a sport as to play a sport.
Ⓒ A randomly chosen student who does not play a sport is 5 times as likely to not play an instrument as to play an instrument.
Ⓓ A randomly chosen student who plays an instrument is 6 times as likely to play a sport as to not play a sport.

10. 150 students were surveyed and asked whether they played a sport and whether they played a musical instrument. The results are shown in the table below.

	Plays an Instrument	Does not Plays an Instrument
Plays a Sport	60	30
Does not Plays a Sport	10	50

Which two sections add up to just over half of the number of students surveyed?

Ⓐ The two sections that do not play an instrument.
Ⓑ The two sections that do not play a sport.
Ⓒ The two sections that play an instrument.
Ⓓ The two sections that play a sport.

11. Match the data with the correct association.

	POSITIVE ASSOCIA-TION	NEGATIVE ASSOCIA-TION	NO ASSOCIATION
The population survey data for 5 years shows the number of goldfish and star fish. Describe the association between the population of goldfish and star fish. <table><tr><td>YEAR</td><td>1</td><td>2</td><td>3</td><td>4</td><td>5</td></tr><tr><td>GOLDFISH</td><td>13</td><td>18</td><td>19</td><td>20</td><td>25</td></tr><tr><td>STARFISH</td><td>30</td><td>25</td><td>20</td><td>15</td><td>12</td></tr></table>	○	○	○
Below is data for 5 years showing Jonny's and Jack's weight in kg. Describe the association between the weight of Jonny and Jack. <table><tr><td>YEAR</td><td>1</td><td>2</td><td>3</td><td>4</td><td>5</td></tr><tr><td>JONNY</td><td>30</td><td>40</td><td>42</td><td>49</td><td>52</td></tr><tr><td>JACK</td><td>30</td><td>35</td><td>40</td><td>45</td><td>50</td></tr></table>	○	○	○
The data for 5 days shows the sale of watermelon and potatoes. Describe the association between the sale of watermelon and potatoes. <table><tr><td>DAYS</td><td>1</td><td>2</td><td>3</td><td>4</td><td>5</td></tr><tr><td>WATERMELON</td><td>70</td><td>26</td><td>60</td><td>19</td><td>70</td></tr><tr><td>POTATO</td><td>10</td><td>40</td><td>15</td><td>80</td><td>22</td></tr></table>	○	○	○

12. Following is 10 days of data which shows the sale of apples and mangoes. Fill in the type of association there is between the apple and mango sales.

DAYS	1	2	3	4	5	6	7	8	9	10
APPLE	62	49	81	26	45	55	16	74	97	34
MANGO	36	44	49	37	26	11	76	83	64	81

There is _____ between apple and mango sale.

13. Fill in the table with the word positive, negative, or none to describe which type of association is plotted.

Scatter Plot	Type of Association

CHAPTER 4 → Lesson 2: Analyzing Linear Scatter Plots

1.

Which of the following scatter plots below demonstrates the same type of data correlation as the one shown above?

Ⓐ

Ⓒ

Ⓑ

Ⓓ

2.

Which of the following lines most accurately models the points in this scatter plot?

Ⓐ

Ⓒ

Ⓑ

Ⓓ

3.

Which of the following lines most accurately models the points in this scatter plot?

Ⓐ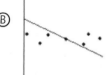

Ⓒ

Ⓑ

Ⓓ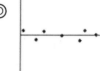

4.

Which of the following lines most accurately models the points in this scatter plot?

Ⓐ

Ⓒ

Ⓑ

Ⓓ

5. The four scatter plots below have all been modeled by the same line. Which scatter plot has the strongest association?

Ⓐ

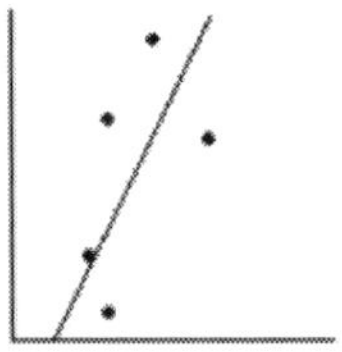

Ⓒ

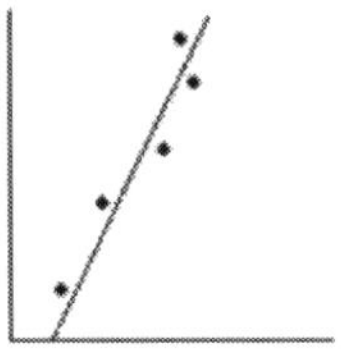

Ⓑ

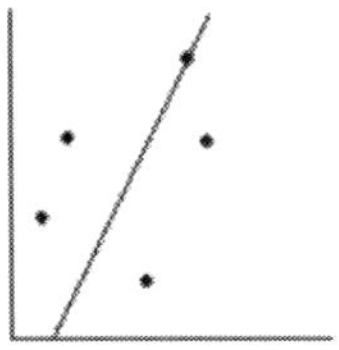

Ⓓ

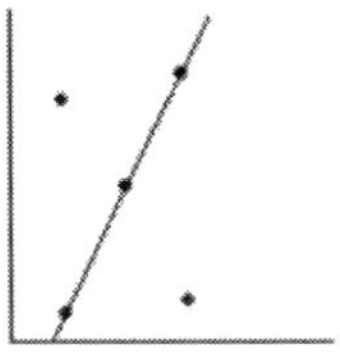

6. The four scatter plots shown below have four points in common, and each scatter plot has a different fifth point. Which scatter plot's fifth point is an outlier?

Ⓐ

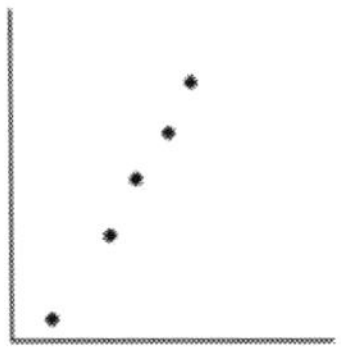

Ⓒ

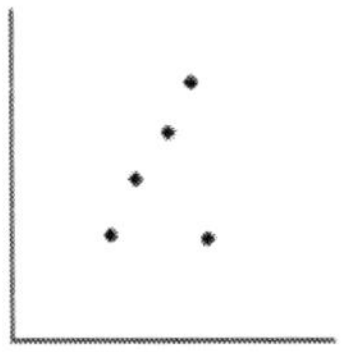

Ⓑ

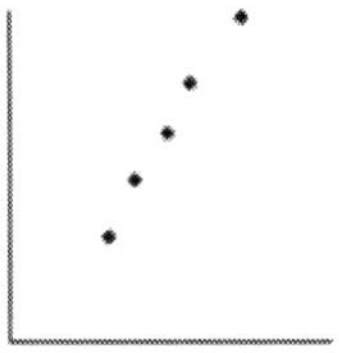

Ⓓ

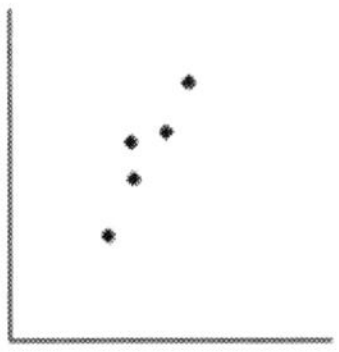

7. The four scatter plots shown below have four points in common, and each scatter plot has a different fifth point. Which scatter plot's fifth point is NOT an outlier?

Ⓐ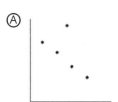

Ⓒ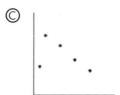

Ⓑ

Ⓓ

8. The figure below shows a scatter plot relating the length of a bean plant, in centimeters, to the number of days since it was planted. The slope of the associated line is 2. Which of the following correctly interprets the slope?

Ⓐ The bean plant grows approximately 1 cm every 2 days.
Ⓑ The bean plant grows approximately 2 cm each day.
Ⓒ The bean plant was 2 cm long when it was planted.
Ⓓ The bean plant approximately doubles in length each day.

9. The figure below shows a scatter plot relating the cost of a ride in a taxicab, in dollars, to the number of miles traveled. The slope of the associated line is 0.5. Which of the following correctly interprets the slope?

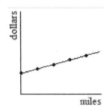

Ⓐ For each additional mile traveled, the cost of the ride increases by 50 cents.
Ⓑ For each additional half of a mile traveled, the cost of the ride increases by 1 dollar.
Ⓒ The initial cost of the ride, before the taxi has traveled any distance, is 50 cents.
Ⓓ The first half of a mile does not cost anything.

10. The figure below shows a scatter plot relating the temperature in a school's parking lot, in degrees Fahrenheit, to the number of hours past noon. The slope of the associated line is -3. Which of the following correctly interprets the slope?

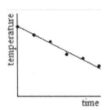

Ⓐ The temperature at noon was -3 degrees Fahrenheit.
Ⓑ The temperature decreased until it reached -3 degrees Fahrenheit.
Ⓒ The temperature decreased an average of 1 degree Fahrenheit every 3 hours.
Ⓓ The temperature decreased an average of 3 degrees Fahrenheit per hour.

LumosLearning.com

11. Match the correct vocab term with the correct definition.

	Linear	Negative Association	Line of Best Fit	Prediction Equation
A line on a graph showing the general direction that a group of points seem to be heading	○	○	○	○
A graph that is represented by a straight line	○	○	○	○
The equation of a line that can predict outcomes using given data	○	○	○	○
A correlation of points that is linear with a negative slope	○	○	○	○

12. Write the equation of the best fit line for this scatter plot using the 2 ordered pairs given.

Write your answer in the box given below.

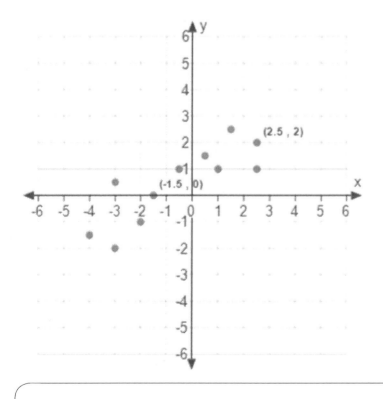

CHAPTER 4 → Lesson 3: Scatter Plots, Line of Best Fit

1.

Which of the following best describes the points in this scatter plot?

Ⓐ **Increasing Linear**
Ⓑ **Decreasing Linear**
Ⓒ **Constant Linear**
Ⓓ **None of these**

2.

Which of the following best describes the points in this scatter plot?

Ⓐ **Increasing Linear**
Ⓑ **Decreasing Linear**
Ⓒ **Constant Linear**
Ⓓ **None of these**

3.

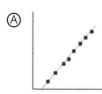

Which of the following lines best approximates the data in the scatter plot shown above?

Ⓐ

Ⓑ

Ⓒ

Ⓓ None of these; the data do not appear to be related linearly.

4. Which scatter plot represents a positive linear association?

Ⓐ

Ⓑ

Ⓒ

Ⓓ

5. **Which scatter plot represents a negative linear association?**

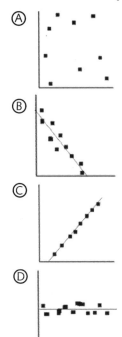

6. **Which scatter plot represents no association?**

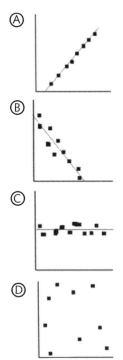

7. Which scatter plot represents a constant association?

Ⓐ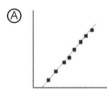

Ⓑ

Ⓒ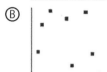

Ⓓ

8. The graph of this data set would most resemble which of the following graphs?

x	1	2	3	4	5	6	7
y	2	3	4	5	6	7	8

Ⓐ

Ⓑ

Ⓒ

Ⓓ

9. The graph of this data would most resemble which of the following graphs?

x	1	2	3	4	5	6	7
y	4	4	4	4	4	4	4

Ⓐ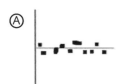

Ⓑ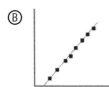

Ⓒ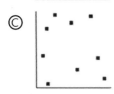

Ⓓ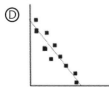

10. Typically air temperature decreases through the night between midnight and 6:00 am. This is an example of what type of association?

Ⓐ constant association
Ⓑ positive linear association
Ⓒ negative linear association
Ⓓ no association

11. Match which line would be the best fit to describe the data pictured.

Figure - 1

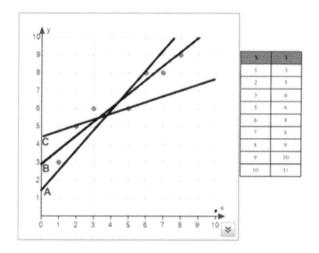

Figure - 2

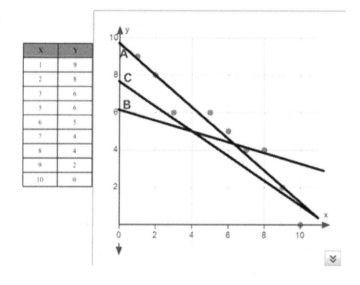

	A	B	C
Figure - 1	○	○	○
Figure - 2	○	○	○

12. Write the prediction equation for this graph using the two labeled points. Leave as fractions.

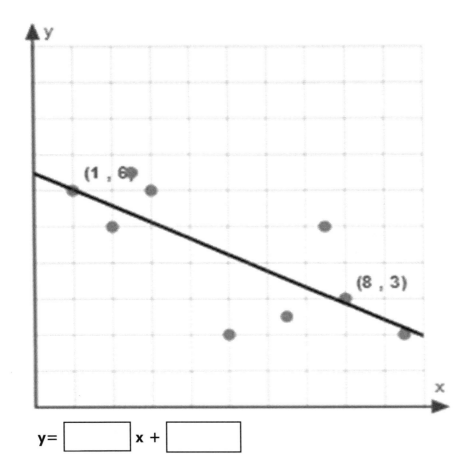

(1 , 6)

(8 , 3)

y = [ ] x + [ ]

13. Cathy wanted to know what kind of shows the 8th grade class preferred – dramas or comedies. 55 students said they liked comedies and not dramas. 25 students liked both dramas and comedies. There were 41 students who did not like dramas nor comedies. Complete a two way table using the information given.

	Doesn't Like Dramas	Likes Dramas	Total
Doesn't Like Comedies	41		97
Likes Comedies		25	
Total	96		177

LumosLearning.com

CHAPTER 4 → Lesson 4: Sample Space of an Experiment

1. **What is the sample space for flipping a fair coin three times?**

   Ⓐ {HHH, HHT, HTH, HTT, THH, THT, TTH, TTT}
   Ⓑ {H, T}
   Ⓒ {HH, HT, TH, TT}
   Ⓓ {HHH, TTT}

2. **Two six-sided fair dice are rolled. How many unique possibilities are there in the sample space?**

   Ⓐ 6
   Ⓑ 12
   Ⓒ 18
   Ⓓ 21

3. **You're flipping a coin until you get heads. What is the sample space?**

   Ⓐ {H, TH, TTH, TTTH, ...}
   Ⓑ {H, T}
   Ⓒ {HH, HT, TH, TT}
   Ⓓ {HHH, TTT}

4. **A spinner has three equal sectors colored red, blue, and green. If the spinner is spun twice, what is the sample space?**

   Ⓐ {RR, BB, GG}
   Ⓑ {RB, RG, BR, BG, GR, GB}
   Ⓒ {R, B, G}
   Ⓓ {RR, BB, GG, RB, RG, BR, BG, GR, GB}

5. **You're rolling a fair six-sided die and flipping a fair coin. What is the sample space?**

   Ⓐ {1H, 2H, ..., 6H, 1T, 2T, ..., 6T}
   Ⓑ {1, 2, 3, 4, 5, 6}
   Ⓒ {HH, HT, TH, TT}
   Ⓓ {H, T}

6. **You're selecting a team of three players from a group of five. What is the sample space?**

    Ⓐ {AAA, BBB, CCC, DDD, EEE}
    Ⓑ {A, B, C, D, E}
    Ⓒ {ABC, ABD, ABE, ACD, ACE, ADE, BCD, BCE, BDE, CDE}
    Ⓓ {AAB, AAC, AAD, AAE, ABB, ACC, ..., EDE, EEE}

7. **You're rolling two fair dice and multiplying the outcomes. What is the sample space?**

    Ⓐ {1, 2, 3, 4, 5, 6, 7, 8, 9, 10, 11, 12}
    Ⓑ {1, 2, 3, 4, 5, 6, 8, 9, 10, 12, 15, 16, 18, 20, 24, 25, 30, 36}
    Ⓒ {11, 12, 21, 22, ..., 66}
    Ⓓ {1, 4, 9, 16, 25, 36}

8. **In a bag, there are 4 red marbles, 3 blue marbles, and 1 green marbles. If you draw two marbles without replacement, list the sample space. Write your answer in the box below.**

9. **A coin is flipped and a die is rolled. What is the number of possible outcomes? Write your answer in the box below.**

10. **A coin is flipped and a card is picked from a regular deck of cards. What is the number of possible outcomes? Write your answer in the box below.**

CHAPTER 4 → Lesson 5: Finding Probability

1. **A fair six-sided die is rolled. What is the probability of rolling a 3?**

   Ⓐ $\frac{1}{3}$

   Ⓑ $\frac{1}{6}$

   Ⓒ $\frac{1}{2}$

   Ⓓ $\frac{2}{3}$

2. **A bag contains 4 red marbles and 6 blue marbles. If a marble is drawn at random, what is the probability of drawing a red marble?**

   Ⓐ $\frac{2}{5}$

   Ⓑ $\frac{4}{10}$

   Ⓒ $\frac{1}{2}$

   Ⓓ $\frac{4}{6}$

3. **A deck of playing cards has 52 cards, with 4 suits (hearts, diamonds, clubs, spades) and 13 ranks in each suit. What is the probability of drawing a king?**

   Ⓐ $\frac{1}{13}$

   Ⓑ $\frac{3}{13}$

   Ⓒ $\frac{1}{4}$

   Ⓓ $\frac{1}{52}$

4. In a bag, there are 8 green marbles, 4 blue marbles, and 3 yellow marbles. If a marble is drawn at random, what is the probability of drawing a blue or a yellow marble?

Ⓐ $\frac{1}{3}$

Ⓑ $\frac{7}{15}$

Ⓒ $\frac{3}{15}$

Ⓓ $\frac{1}{2}$

5. A spinner is divided into 8 equal sections, numbered from 1 to 8. What is the probability of spinning an even number?

Ⓐ $\frac{1}{2}$

Ⓑ $\frac{3}{8}$

Ⓒ $\frac{4}{7}$

Ⓓ $\frac{2}{8}$

6. A box contains 20 candies: 12 chocolate and 8 vanilla. If a candy is chosen at random, what is the probability of choosing a vanilla candy?

Ⓐ $\frac{2}{5}$

Ⓑ $\frac{3}{5}$

Ⓒ $\frac{8}{20}$

Ⓓ $\frac{40}{100}$

7. A deck of cards is shuffled well. What is the probability of drawing a red card or a face card (jack, queen, king)?

Ⓐ $\frac{8}{13}$

Ⓑ $\frac{17}{52}$

Ⓒ $\frac{3}{13}$

Ⓓ $\frac{11}{26}$

8. In a bag, there are 5 white marbles and 7 black marbles. If a marble is drawn at random, what is the probability of not drawing a black marble?

   Ⓐ $\frac{1}{2}$

   Ⓑ $\frac{5}{12}$

   Ⓒ $\frac{7}{12}$

   Ⓓ $\frac{1}{3}$

9. A box contains 10 red, 12 blue and 15 green balls. If a ball is chosen at random, what is the probability of choosing a red ball or a green ball?

   Ⓐ $\frac{12}{37}$

   Ⓑ $\frac{27}{37}$

   Ⓒ $\frac{25}{37}$

   Ⓓ $\frac{22}{37}$

10. A standard deck of cards is shuffled well. What is the probability of drawing a heart or a queen

   Ⓐ $\frac{9}{56}$

   Ⓑ $\frac{4}{13}$

   Ⓒ $\frac{17}{52}$

   Ⓓ $\frac{1}{4}$

End of Data Analysis and Probability

Notes

Additional Information

Test Taking Tips

1) **The day before the test,** make sure you get a good night's sleep.
2) **On the day of the test,** be sure to eat a good hearty breakfast! Also, be sure to arrive at school on time.
3) **During the test:**

- **Read every question carefully.**
  - Do not spend too much time on any one question. Work steadily through all questions in the section.
  - Attempt all of the questions even if you are not sure of some answers.
  - If you run into a difficult question, eliminate as many choices as you can and then pick the best one from the remaining choices. Intelligent guessing will help you increase your score.
  - Also, mark the question so that if you have extra time, you can return to it after you reach the end of the section.
  - Some questions may refer to a graph, chart, or other kind of picture. Carefully review the graphic before answering the question.
  - Be sure to include explanations for your written responses and show all work.

- **While Answering EBSR questions.**
  - EBSR questions come in 2 parts - PART A and B.
  - Both PART A and B could be multiple choice or Part A could be multiple choice while Part B could be some other type.
  - Generally, Part A and B will be related, sometimes it may just be from the same lesson but not related questions.
  - If it is a Multiple choice question, Select the bubble corresponding to your answer choice.
  - Read all of the answer choices, even if think you have found the correct answer.
  - In case the questions in EBSR are not multiple choice questions, follow the instruction for other question types while answering such questions.

- **While Answering TECR questions.**
  - Read the directions of each question. Some might ask you to drag something, others to select, and still others to highlight. Follow all instructions of the question (or questions if it is in multiple parts)

Frequently Asked Questions(FAQs)

For more information on 2023-24 Assessment Year, visit
www.lumoslearning.com/a/fast-faqs
OR Scan the **QR Code**

Progress Chart

Standard	Lesson	Score	Date of Completion
BEST			
MA.8.NSO.1.1	Rational vs. Irrational Numbers		
MA.8.NSO.1.2	Approximating Irrational Numbers		
MA.8.NSO.1.3	Properties of Exponents		
MA.8.NSO.1.4 MA.8.NSO.1.5	Scientific Notations		
MA.8.NSO.1.6	Solving Problems Involving Scientific Notation		
MA.8.NSO.1.7	Square & Cube Roots		
MA.8.AR.1.2	Multiplying Linear Expressions		
MA.8.AR.1.3	Factorizing Algebraic Expressions		
MA.8.AR.2.1	Solving Linear Equations		
MA.8.AR.2.1	Solve Linear Equations with Rational Numbers		
MA.8.AR.2.2	Two-step Linear Inequalities		
MA.8.AR.3.1	Proportional Relationships		
MA.8.AR.3.2	Compare Proportions		
MA.8.AR.3.3	Understanding Slope		
MA.8.AR.3.4	Expressing Linear Equations		
MA.8.AR.3.5	Interpreting Slope		
MA.8.AR.4.1	Solving Systems of Equations		
MA.8.AR.4.2	Solutions to Systems of Equations		
MA.8.AR.4.3	Systems of Equations in Real-World Problems		

Standard	Lesson	Score	Date of Completion
BEST			
MA.8.GR.1.1	Pythagorean Theorem in Real-World Problems		
MA.8.GR.1.2	Pythagorean Theorem & Coordinate System		
MA.8.GR.1.3	Verifying the Pythagorean Theorem		
MA.8.GR.1.4	Angles		
MA.8.GR.1.5	Interior & Exterior Angles in Geometric Figures		
MA.8.GR.1.6	Interior Angles of Regular Polygons		
MA.8.GR.2.1	Transformations of Points & Lines		
MA.8.GR.2.1	Transformations of Angles		
MA.8.GR.2.1	Transformations of Parallel Lines		
MA.8.GR.2.2	Transformations of Congruency		
MA.8.GR.2.3	Analyzing Transformations		
MA.8.GR.2.4	Transformations & Similarity		
MA.8.DP.1.1	Interpreting Data Tables & Scatter Plots		
MA.8.DP.1.2	Analyzing Linear Scatter Plots		
MA.8.DP.1.3	Scatter Plots, Line of Best Fit		
MA.8.DP.2.1	Sample Space of an Experiment		
MA.8.DP.2.2 MA.8.DP.2.3	Finding Probability		

Grade 8

Lumos Learning
Step Up Your Skills

FLORIDA
ENGLISH
LANGUAGE ARTS LITERACY

Aligned with B.E.S.T. Standards

FAST Practice

Student Copy

(((tedBook)))
ONLINE

2 Practice Tests
Personalized Study Plan

ELA Strands Reading • Communication • Vocabulary

Available
- At Leading book stores
- Online www.LumosLearning.com

Made in the USA
Columbia, SC
29 August 2024

40817813R00080